BUILDING THE ULTIMATE NETWORK

Published by CelebrityPress™, Orlando, FL
A division of The Celebrity Branding Agency®

Celebrity Branding® is a registered trademark
Printed in the United States of America.

ISBN: 9780983340485
LCCN: 2011932405

This publication is designed to provide accurate and authoritative information with regard to the subject matter covered. It is sold with the understanding that the publisher is not engaged in rendering legal, accounting, or other professional advice. If legal advice or other expert assistance is required, the services of a competent professional should be sought. The opinions expressed by the authors in this book are not endorsed by CelebrityPress™ and are the sole responsibility of the author rendering the opinion.

Most CelebrityPress™ titles are available at special quantity discounts for bulk purchases for sales promotions, premiums, fundraising, and educational use. Special versions or book excerpts can also be created to fit specific needs.

For more information, please write:

CelebrityPress™,
520 N. Orlando Ave, #2
Winter Park, FL 32789

or call 1.877.261.4930

Visit us online at www.**CelebrityPressPublishing**.com

BUILDING THE
ULTIMATE
NETWORK

The World's Leading Entrepreneurs Reveal Their Top Secrets
for Building Profitable Relationships Online and Offline

TABLE OF CONTENTS

FOREWORD

WHY MAKE ALL THE MISTAKES, WHEN WE CAN LEARN FROM OTHERS?

BY DR. IVAN MISNER

There are "tried-and–true" networking techniques that are so simplistic they seem that they cannot be really effective. Many times, we try to re-evaluate, improve upon and complicate them. An experience I had once, while on vacation, reminds me of how we try to make some things harder than they really are.

I was in Hawaii enjoying the surf when, unbeknownst to me, the water became thick with Portuguese Man O'War jellyfish. Suddenly I felt a stinging sensation across my chest. I wiped my chest with my right wrist and arm and lifted my arm up out of the water. I saw the tentacles dripping off my arm and followed them with my eyes about 8 feet away to the body of the Man O'War jellyfish. With mounting alarm, I shook the tentacles off my wrist back into the water and quickly swam out of the surf to the shore.

I ran up to the first hotel employee I saw, a cabana boy, who was serving drinks to a sunning couple just off the pool deck and urgently exclaimed, "I think I've just been hit in the chest by a Man O'War jellyfish! What should I do??"

"Are you feeling any pressure in your chest?" he wanted to know.

"No, none at all," I replied anxiously.

"Okay, okay, here's what you need to do. Go on over to the market off the lobby and ask for some vinegar and meat tenderizer. You're going to want to spray the vinegar onto your chest and then shake the meat tenderizer onto the same spot and rub it all around. You'll be fine," he assured me.

Well, I must say that I was less than impressed with this bizarre advice. He was entirely too calm and that was entirely too easy to be a real solution – not to mention that it was just plain strange. I figured he was doing a version of "let's goof on the tourist," so I moved on to ask someone else for help.

I spotted a hotel employee standing not too far off and gingerly jogged over to him, urgently repeating my exclamation, "I've just been hit in the chest by a Man O'War jellyfish; what should I do?"

He said, "Are you feeling any pressure in your chest?" Oh boy, I thought, next he's going to tell me to get some meat tenderizer! I thought he was kidding, or maybe I was in a bad dream and just couldn't wake up.

"No, I'm not feeling any pressure in my chest," I reluctantly responded.

"Okay, then go over to the market off the lobby and ask for some vinegar and meat tenderizer. You have to get that on your chest and rub it around and then you'll be just fine," he said reassured. I felt anything but reassured.

By this time, I thought that maybe I better find someone who might really know what to do. I headed up to the lobby, thinking that the hotel manager would be a good choice for a straight answer.

There at the front desk was a mature gentleman wearing a badge that read: "Hotel Manager." Surely, I thought, this guy's not going to "goof on the tourist." I walked up to him and repeated my mantra about the jellyfish strike. He looked at me with grave concern and said, "Are you feeling any pressure in your chest." "No," I replied, "I'm not feeling any chest pain." "OK, good," he said. "You need to go down the hall to the small market and get some vinegar and meat tenderizer and put them on one at a time and rub them thoroughly into your chest."

Finally, I said what I'd been thinking all along… "You can't be serious, right?" "This is a joke, right?" "No," he reassured me this was not a joking matter. I needed to proceed to the store immediately and apply that remedy.

I reluctantly trucked down the hall to the store just knowing that they were all back there laughing at the goofy tourist who was actually going to do a self-imposed "meat rub" on his chest. I was sure they had some barbecue grill going for when I returned to the lobby all slathered up with vinegar and meat tenderizer.

I entered the small market off the lobby and started my search for char-grilled products when I started feeling short of breath. Suddenly, very quickly and forcefully, I began to experience a crushing weight on my chest. Was I having a heart attack? Great! I'm having a coronary after wasting so much time talking to members of the hotel staff, who were trying to get me to rub meat tenderizer on my chest. I walked out of the store and staggered to the front desk, which by now was very busy with new guests checking in to the hotel. I made eye contact with the hotel manager and almost immediately, dropped to the ground, clutching my chest, barely able to gasp "Man O'War!"

What happened next was a total blur. I seem to remember a small child yelling and pointing at me as I lay there in my bathing suit, gasping for breath.

"Look mommy, there's a man on the floor." The mother said something about staying away from people who do drugs. I looked over and tried to say no, not drugs – jellyfish! But all that came out was gibberish.

The paramedics rushed to the scene. Finally, I was going to get the medical attention I needed. After determining what had happened, the paramedic opened his life-saving kit and I knew he was about to pull out a defibrillator. I made my peace with God and I braced myself for the big jolt. Instead, he pulled out – yes, you guessed it – vinegar in a spray bottle and some Adolf's meat tenderizer! He then proceeded to spray the vinegar and then sprinkle the meat tenderizer on my chest, and thoroughly rub the mixture around. Within seconds, literally seconds, the excruciating pain began to subside. Within a couple minutes it was almost completely gone.

What I thought was a big "barbeque joke" on the tourist turns out to be a well-known cure for some jellyfish strikes. You see, the meat tenderizer contains the enzyme papain, which breaks down the toxin proteins and neutralizes them. It sounds too simple to be really effective, but it is, in fact, one of the best things to do in that situation.

Thinking back on it, I am amazed at how many people gave me the solution before I had to learn the hard way. Sure, who's going to believe a cabana boy? I mean, what does he know, right? And the hotel employee – OK, maybe there's the start of a pattern here but, I have a doctoral degree – I'm "smart," and these guys have just got to be kidding me... right? And then the hotel manager as well... OK, I admit it, at that point there's just no excuse. I should have figured out these guys knew what they were talking about and I did not.

I made one of the biggest mistakes that people in business make – I didn't listen to the people who have experience. I assumed that I just had to know better... and the truth is, I didn't know better.

There is nothing like experience. It beats education every day of the week. The only thing better is a combination of education and experience... or a willingness to learn from other people's experience. There are many basic referral marketing and networking techniques that any good businessperson knows to be effective. They don't try to look for something more complicated or involved, because they know from their own experience, as well as the experience of others, what works in business and what doesn't work in business.

Throughout this book you may read things that seem too simple to be effective, or you may see ideas that you've heard before. Don't dismiss them. Embrace them. Although these ideas may be simple – they are not easy. If it they were easy, everyone would do them – and they don't! Great networkers learn from other people's success. So, go get that vinegar and meat tenderizer and learn from other "masters" that sometimes the simplest ideas can have the biggest impact.

Called the father of modern networking by CNN, Dr. Ivan Misner is a New York Times bestselling author. He is the Founder and Chairman of BNI (www.bni.com), the world's largest business networking organization.

You can read more of his material on his blog at: www.BusinessNetworking.com.

Dr. Misner is also the Sr. Partner for the Referral Institute, an international referral training company: www.referralinstitute.com

CHAPTER I

SUCCESSFUL NETWORKING IS AN INSIDE JOB

BY EMORY G. COWAN JR., PHD

The person who coined the term "Workaholic" was my colleague, pastoral theologian and medical school professor, Wayne Oates. One day Dr. Oates was franticly making his way through the Birmingham, Alabama airport, trying to get to his plane before the doors closed. Running down the crowded concourse, he hurriedly pushed past two men. When one of them said, "Hey mister, don't hurry," the directive caught Dr. Oates by surprise, so he stopped suddenly, turned around and said, "Why?" "Because we are the pilots of your flight!" one of the men responded (Oates, 1971, p.92). The first time I heard him tell this story, even though I had read it in his book, I laughed like everyone else, but then I was struck with how much it spoke to my sense of hurry and working hard to be successful. I had a strong awareness of how out-of-touch I was getting with the people I needed most.

You and I need other people to support us, nurture us, and connect us to the world of relationships and business, even though at times we all have said, "I don't need anybody else, I can do it by myself!" How we delude ourselves into thinking that if we work harder, and run faster, we can make our lives and our work successful. As entrepreneurial people, we often become so busy that we think we don't have time to slow down. We wind up leaving our pilots, our network, behind.

I really believe that successful networking is an *inside* job. In order to be successful at developing a network of business professionals, the starting place is with our self. We must examine what it is about our self that attracts or repels the confidence and trust of others. We need to learn to slow down so we can really listen to people, and we must learn how to nurture the relationships that are vital to our success.

In our society, we also delude ourselves into thinking that appearance counts for far more than any other factor in attracting other people. YAVIS people (Young, Attractive, Verbal, Intelligent, and Successful individuals) seem to be accepted into groups more readily, and they appear to be more successful than others at getting jobs, creating wealth, developing friendships and enjoying the good life. This explains why our cultural heroes are often those in the entertainment industry or sport fields. YAVIS people appear to have self-confidence and the loyalty of others, and can get everything they want out of life. So when they fall, due to some moral, ethical, or legal breach, we are dismayed.

The truth is, being a YAVIS person does not ensure a successful network or ultimate success in life. Abraham Lincoln was not an attractive person (… someone once said that he was the homeliest man he had ever seen), and he suffered from many personal business and relationship failures. But there was something else about Lincoln that inspired people to follow him. Specifically, his honesty and integrity inspired trust and loyalty from people. Although Lincoln had suffered personal losses, and enormous grief, he had a keen sense of self and was a centered person. *He knew who he was and he knew how to treat people with respect.*

You don't have to be a YAVIS person to have a successful following of people, but there are some things you must attend to in order to get there.

GET TO KNOW YOURSELF

Trust me; there are aspects of your personality that others readily see and know about that are completely unknown to you.

Sometime in 1968, a tour bus turned on to Haight-Ashbury Street in San Francisco. The gawking middle-age tourists were shocked at the scene of the "Flower Children" who had taken over the district. When the bus stopped at the traffic light, a crazy-looking, bare-chested young man with wild flowing red hair ran to the bus and held up a mirror to the shocked passengers. As he walked down the line of windows, passengers were forced to look at themselves.

Plato reported that Socrates admonished those who followed him that *to be wise,* you must "Know Thyself." I believe that the first step toward being a successful networker, and perhaps the most difficult, is to know yourself. As a psychotherapist, I spent many years in personal therapy trying to know myself, so my "self stuff" wouldn't get in the way of other people's journey to discover their 'self.' In addition, I tried to surround myself with friends and colleagues who would speak the truth to me. Why? It is because we all have a significant "blind spot" in our lives. Trust me; there are aspects of your personality that others readily see and know about us that are completely unknown to you. It is those unknown things, our personal blind spot, which may be an impediment to relationship building. Your blind spot may be expressed in the way you talk to other people, your behaviors toward others, or simply the non-verbal expressions you display.

I once had a client who was one of the most intelligent and gifted individuals I have ever known. This person's storehouse of knowledge and insight into the world of business was far beyond that of her peers. Nevertheless, she had a blind spot that led to multiple failures in her marriage and business relationships. To her great dismay, she could not develop a viable and sustainable network of people. She left a trail of relationship disasters in her wake. The reason? In her early childhood, she suffered such a terrible abandonment experience that she always came across as a needy, empty person. To compensate for her neediness, she approached people in an overly solicitous and ingratiating manner. At the same time, she acted as a pompous know-it-all, which, as you can imagine, turned people off almost immediately. Her problem was that having a great emptiness in her personality caused her to try to fill it with other people. And other people resent being treated like an object. Nevertheless, with a little hard work in therapy, she was able to gain some insight and modify her behavior. She tried to stop using other people, and by changing that one thing, she avoided damaging subsequent relationships. As a result, she learned to treat others with the same care that she wanted for herself, and her business network began to flourish.

LEARN TO REALLY LISTEN

If we don't know ourselves, our needs and boundaries, then it becomes easy to treat other people as if they were mere objects in our world, filling the void in our lives. A Realtor I know is a sharp dresser and drives an expensive car, but you can count the number of people who genuinely respect him on two or three fingers. Why? He uses people for his own gain and neglects the fact that other people have feelings and needs. For him, people are simply a means to an end, and the end is always, "what's in it for me!" Although he has made some money, the amount would be many times more than what he has realized, if he knew how to empathize with, and show genuine positive regard for, others. Mr. "All Business" likes to tell others what a great business man he is. He enjoys bragging about his accomplishments, and in doing so he has made a reputation for himself. He relates to other people as if they are objects in his world, so there is no depth in his business network. Potential networkers figure out pretty quickly that he doesn't have time for them, and that he is not really interested in their lives.

Mr. "All Business" never discovered the secret that everybody has a story to tell, and we all want someone to listen to us. You might be surprised what sitting down with another person and genuinely listening to their story will do for a relationship, business or otherwise. Dr. Ivan Misner, founder of the world's largest networking organization, BNI, constantly reminds his Directors that they have two ears and one mouth and should govern themselves accordingly.

One popular method of communication skills training is called "active listening." The method trains people to respond by reflecting back to the speaker what the listener has heard. The goal is a search for the meaning of what is being said by seeking clarification of the process. That is accomplished by reframing and restating what the listener has heard the speaker say. The result is that the speaker's experience is one of being heard, understood, and validated. All of us want people to really hear us and to understand us.

Sadly, the fact is that most of the time we hear only a small percentage of what is actually said to us. In addition, much of the time we are completely unaware of a person's non-verbal communication. That is of great concern because the majority of communication is non-verbal. At one time in my career, I conducted communication training for first year medical residents in a large teaching hospital. The goal was to teach them how to actively listen to the verbal and non- verbal communication of their patients. They need to know that many of the words in our language have several different meanings, and unless we clarify with the speaker what is being said to us, we may miss the meaning the speaker attaches to the word. In addition, I tried to demonstrate to these young physicians that perhaps as much as 75-80% of communication to them is non-verbal. It is not so much the words we use as it is the gestures, the inflection, and the use of facial muscles. The popular television series, "Lie To Me" uses the real life technology of micro facial muscle movements that was developed in the 1960s and 70s by Dr John Gottman and others, to depict it's stories of individual emotions and veracity as displayed on the faces of the actors.

To really communicate effectively, a good business person must learn to read between the lines, look for the meaning of words spoken, understand facial muscle movements, and be aware of the meaning of other non-verbal gestures. Mastering communication sets the stage for the third aspect of making your network successful.

NURTURE YOUR NETWORK

Every year, with the approach of spring, I get a very primitive urge to plant a garden. It is one of the residuals of growing up on a farm. So, as the weather warms, I check the calendar for the best time to plant. I get out my tools, till the soil, fertilize it, and look for the best seed or seedlings. Last year my garden grew and was thriving until a family emergency arose and I had to be away from home for several weeks. You can imagine what happens to a robust garden of squash, tomatoes, beans, broccoli, and okra when you fail to weed it; you can imagine what happens when you turn off the water sup-ply. When I returned home after several weeks, to what should have been a good harvest, all I found were plants that had withered and died.

The same thing happens to relationships if you are not intentional about pre-paring, pruning, weeding, and watering them. They die! Although I strongly believe that there is a mystery in how and why relationships get started, I am equally convinced that to sustain them you must work continuously to nurture them.

Just today I received a letter from a financial advisor of mine. As his customers, he constantly maintains contact with my wife and me through phone calls, birthday cards, letters, and one-to-one visits. He does that for all his clients, and he also does it with his network of business associates who sustain him with referrals. What a novel idea! He treats his network with the same care that he gives his best clients. And you can too.

WHAT CAN YOU DO?

The three step process that I have set out is one that you can begin to apply today as action steps. If you will act on them, your network will be successful. Another way of saying this is that your network will be as successful as you choose to make it. So, no excuses! If you want to develop a viable, successful, and sustainable network, it is really quite simple: (A) Get to know yourself; (B) Learn to really listen; and (C) Nurture your networkers. Here are some things you can do to make it happen.

1. **See a psychotherapist or a counselor.** You don't have to be crazy or mentally ill to see a therapist. As I said previously, all of us have blind spots which affect our relationships. A good professional counselor can be that mirror for you to help you see yourself and the way that you relate to other people, more accurately.

2. **Take a course in active listening skills or other communication skills training.** Learning how to communicate effectively can't hurt your business, it can only increase the opportunities to develop more depth of relationships and trust from your business networkers. Check with the CPA in your network to see if you can write it off as a business expense.

3. **Develop a system to regularly contact and nurture your net.** Just as "Location, Location, Location" is the slogan for the Real Estate industry, "Nurture, Nurture, Nurture" is the key to cultivating and sustaining relationships. With state-of-the-art computer software, you can create ways to treat your network members with the same care and concern that you would give to your best client.

References
Oates, W. (1971). *Confessions of a workaholic: The facts about work addiction.* New York: World Publishing.

ABOUT EMORY

Emory G. Cowan, Jr., PhD is a psychotherapist, educator, New York Times bestselling author, and entrepreneur. An Army combat veteran of the Vietnam War, he has lived in several countries and traveled extensively throughout the world. He has a PhD in Psychology, is a Marriage and Family Therapist, and was President/CEO of a graduate school for ten years.

Emory is an Executive Director and owner of BNI of Colorado and Southeast Wyoming. He has served BNI International on its Founder's Circle and its International Franchise Advisory Board.

With his wife Margie, Emory makes his home in Colorado where they enjoy the mountain grandeur and visits from their grandchildren. They also live part-time in the Los Angeles, California area.

CHAPTER 2

CONFERENCES BUILD DATABASES, GENERATE REFERRALS

BY ED CRAINE

Y ou are probably looking for the next greatest way to expand the recognition of your company and to set yourself apart from the competition.

You may be a small firm or one of the giants in your industry. You have expertise, satisfied clients, great solutions and outcomes, and a loyal following. You may not have enough people who know about you. You want to create a lasting impression and greater recognition among your key audiences.

Of course, you can advertise in the newspaper or on TV and radio. You can also send out direct mail. There is a place for both of these marketing strategies. I've used these and other strategies, but have also added a challenging, yet highly effective element—organizing and hosting conferences. My small award-winning mortgage company had the same marketing challenges that many others are currently facing. The question we asked ourselves was, "How can we do something that would distinguish us from our competitors both large and small in our marketplace?" We decided that the best thing we could do to distinguish ourselves and grow our commercial mortgage business would be to host conferences on timely, valuable, and practical subject matter. We've been doing these for several years now, and the results have been remarkable.

We have built our database by adding several thousand conference attendees to it. More importantly, we have developed new relationships, deepened our relationships with existing clients and referral sources, received many referrals, and best of all 'closed' business as a result of our conference initiative.

So how can you do this? Follow these steps and you too can have a successful conference, no matter what your business is.

ESTABLISH MEANINGFUL GOALS

The absolute number one key to success is determining your purpose and goals for having a conference. In our case, we thought it would be an ideal way to generate recognition as the experts in the commercial sector of our marketplace (–note that we also operate a residential loan division). While many commercial mortgage loan originators hold shorter seminars for commercial real estate agents and investors, we knew that few (and none in our marketplace) were organizing all-day conferences. We realized it would take a major commitment on our part, but that the results could be significant.

We initially had three primary goals:

1. **Obtain clients.** Many of those attending our conferences are interested in investing in a commercial property, either on a short- or long-term basis and most will need a commercial mortgage at some point. Our goal was not necessarily to sell somebody our services right away, but rather to enter into a long-term dialogue. We know that while there may be some "immediate" business opportunities, most of the major deals occur over a longer period of time.

2. **Expand contacts.** Often a more immediate payoff is the development and deepening of relationships with strategic

partners --conference participants-- and attendees. They often become sources of referrals or leads for future programs. The referral sources include commercial real estate agents, CPA's, attorneys, architects, and others with clients interested in commercial real estate opportunities, as well as other lenders and loan originators who may not be able to handle commercial financing. Expanding your prospect/partner database is the prime reason to hold such conferences. We begin this process by obtaining prospects' information on an online reservation form, which we then convert to an Excel file and ultimately upload to our database.

3. **Build our reputation.** Of course, these conferences provide a great forum at which we can demonstrate our expertise. More often than not, people attribute expert status to those who organize and speak at well-thought-out and organized conferences.

For each of these categories we had specific measurable, quantitative goals. You should too.

CREATE A BUDGET

Once you have established your basic goals, you must develop a realistic budget. While you may refine this several times before the conference, you need a starting point. Obviously, the two key components are costs and revenue. In the cost column you will include:

- Hotel space
- Meals/refreshment (which might be in package with hotel space)
- Speaker fees if any
- Handout materials
- Promotional expense

Under the revenue column, you will list:

- Attendees reservation fees
- Sponsorships

A critical part of your budget is determining whether or not you seek to make a profit. Our goal is to break-even on the event. While this type of conference can definitely be a money-maker, our key objectives remain obtaining clients, expanding our contacts, and visibility and credibility. For most of our regular programs, we usually charge $200-300 per attendee to cover expenses. We have found that even in the most difficult economy, most commercial lending and real estate professionals are willing and able to pay to attend a conference, *as long as they feel the content warrants it.*

We have had a few larger conferences that have included a trade show exhibit hall. In such instances, we often have co-sponsors and exhibitor fees that cover the total costs. Our exhibitor fees ranged from $750 to $2,500. While this can be a powerful business development strategy, I recommend that first time conference organizers keep it simple—without a trade show component.

As soon as you have a final list of your projected expenses, you can take a reality check of your proposed budget. First, make a conservative estimate of your expected attendance and multiply that by your planned registration fee. If it seems the total income falls short of the total cost, you need to make some adjustments. On the revenue side, raise the fee, find more sponsors, or increase the conference attendance through greater promotional activities. On the expense side, review and reconsider what expenses you will incur. For example, you could eliminate coffee and beverage service, eliminate or scale-back food service, change your AV requirements, etc.

CHOOSE A THEME AND NAME

To ensure an optimum turnout, it's imperative to create an overall focus that is informative, and themes/topics that will interest the audience. We have emphasized two different approaches based on our business model (yours will differ):

(a). Commercial Lending and investing opportunities: An in-depth look at current trends, opportunities, challenges and "step-by-step" guidelines for closing more business in the commercial property arena. It covers a wide area—from apartment buildings, to office complexes, etc. but the content and principles are universally applicable to all property types, and all professions related to commercial lending and investing.

(b). Strip Mall Financing—This focuses on small strip-retail properties of 5,000 to 50,000 square feet, one of our specialties. We cover topics of interest to owners and professionals dealing with this property type. Topics like leasing issues, management issues, new revenue opportunities, market trends, and financing (of course!).

For each conference we select a name that conveys a valuable reason for real estate professionals and investors to attend. For example, we called one of them *Commercial Distressed Assets and Opportunities*. It wasn't exceptionally creative, but did suggest that attendees would learn of investment opportunities in today's challenging real estate market, which was a major incentive to attend.

Prior to holding our first conference, we surveyed commercial real estate professionals for the type of specific content that they would find most appealing. We discussed several overall subjects—such as the current market conditions and lending sources, as well as a series of subtopics. This feedback was invaluable as it helped us shape the conference and select the speakers. Since then, we have gained sufficient experience in conference planning to most likely know when a topic will "work," although we still seek input from associates and others through a variety of means. Never assume you know it all!

ADAPT THE FORMAT TO THE MARKET

A key initial step is determining whether or not you will have a half-day or full-day conference, or some other format. We have done some of each. Full-day conferences may seem like twice the work as a half-day program, and in some ways they are. However, much of the basic work—securing a hotel/other location, promotion and related preparation is already done. The major difference is the content—arranging additional speakers to fit the afternoon schedule.

You want to develop a program that has a mix of elements. We usually combine programs with both speaker panels and individual presenters. The format is similar to other conferences: morning coffee/get acquainted, welcome address (which I usually make), a panel presentation, coffee break, speaker, lunch, and afternoon speakers.

We strive to provide interactive programs; encouraging attendees to share their experiences during breakout/other sessions and always providing ample time for questions/answers.

Depending on the varied backgrounds of attendees, you may want to offer breakout sessions that are aimed at different interests and experience levels. Of course, this usually entails the need for additional rooms (and cost) and more speaker coordination.

Networking opportunities are another staple of a successful conference. Morning continental breakfast, coffee breaks and lunch are ideal networking options for a half-day program. You can add a late afternoon cocktail reception for a full-day program. We have found that the most popular networking sessions are coffee breaks and luncheons. Many people prefer not to arrive for early breakfast or stay late for a cocktail hour. Of course, refreshment breaks add another level of planning and food and beverage cost to your budget.

As you firm up your basic format, you will start outlining the specific agenda and promote it to prospective participants. Conference attendees are often enticed by the agenda. We try to set the tone by starting with a dynamic keynote presentation. It's also important to keep the conference relatively fast-paced.

INVITE SPEAKERS

Many people are motivated to attend conferences at least partially by the speakers they will hear. You can have a mix of your industry leaders and motivational experts and others. Certainly much of your speaker roster will depend on fees they seek and your overall budget.

I believe the best draw is a group of speakers who are expert practitioners in their area, but not necessarily well-known/highly-recognizable speakers. Potential attendees are impressed that they will learn from some of the most successful, knowledgeable practitioners in the particular area. Speakers like this who provide practical advice and "real world" strategies are generally the most popular. And a bonus for you as an organizer is that they will speak at no cost in return for the market exposure. Some will even pay for a sponsorship to assure higher visibility.

Whatever the combination of speakers you decide on, be sure to conduct your due diligence:

- Get references from groups where speaker has previously appeared.
- Listen to podcasts/other audio of past presentations when available.
- Confirm their general topic—make sure there are no surprises.
- Receive and review PowerPoint presentations in advance.

This basic research is often overlooked. One poor speaker can often put a damper on an otherwise successful conference.

MAKE THE LOCATION CONVENIENT

Although our basic markets are the San Francisco/Sacramento, Calif. areas, we have expanded our commercial lending network. We have also held successful conferences in Los Angeles, where we have strong contacts and potential investors. In addition, we tested our conference strategy in Miami and Phoenix. While these programs were reasonably well attended, we realized we had strayed a little far out of our comfort zone, as we didn't have an extensive database of "local" speakers and attendees as we do our primary market.

Major hotels with the appropriate meeting facilities have been the best venue for our programs, because they are generally flexible enough to meet our space and budget requirements. When looking for a cost effective and convenient site, you may get some good suggestions from Chamber of Commerce or Hotel/Motel Association. You want it to be as close to your core audience as possible. And be sure to choose the quality of venue that is most appropriate to your target audience.

SPONSORS CAN HELP

Having one or more sponsors can not only help balance the budget—by helping to fund the conference—but also help generate more interest. Sponsors will market your conference to their database as well. When looking for a sponsor, you should seek organizations that:

- Are well known in the industry.

- Have a unique product or service that complements your conference focus.
- Have sponsored other conferences, events.
- Will be committed to making your conference a success.

You can enlist support of sponsors that provide financial support as well as those that offer in-kind assistance. The latter typically are media outlets and trade associations that can include announcing the conference to the sponsor's database.

MARKET EFFECTIVELY AND THEY WILL COME

Proactive marketing is an absolute necessity. When we planned our first conference we made sure to promote it in a variety of ways:

➢ Mailed invitations
➢ E-mail blasts
➢ Website announcements

We have since refined our approach, primarily because we have developed a large database of potential attendees. We now generate interest primarily by sending a series of e-mail announcements. Our website (www.commerciallendingconference.com) also helps to create visibility.

Depending on your creativity and budget, you can expand your promotional efforts with:

➢ Facebook announcements
➢ Twitter reminders
➢ Updates for various professional group newsletters

ENHANCE YOUR DATABASE

As already emphasized, the prime reason for holding these conferences is expanding your database. In addition to gathering basic information on the online reservation form, we collect business cards throughout the conference. You may also choose to obtain the basic data via credit card scanners and business card scanners

However, it's critical to also enhance the quality of your conference database information. This involves more onsite "homework" but is well worth the effort. For example, during the conference there are ample networking opportunities to speak with attendees and speakers about their current and future plans, special challenges and other valuable information. You can note such details on their business cards or a small notepad and later add the information to their database profile.

DON'T FORGET TO FOLLOW-UP

Follow-up is critical, on both a short-term and long-term basis. Most immediately, within a few days you need to respond to all of your conference participants. We send attendees a 'thank you' letter and a survey asking for their impressions of the conference. We often include a free gift, such as a software program that helps evaluate commercial properties. We have been fortunate to receive a 40 percent plus response rate on most of these surveys. The input received helps us to determine how to further refine the conference model: the number and types of speakers, venue, handouts, and so on.

We continue to maintain contact with those attendees and other participants who appear to be potential clients, referral partners or other valuable resources. We send letters and other information that will be helpful for their evaluation of commercial properties. In addition, personal meetings are often the best type of follow-up. For example, I welcome the chance for a post-conference get-together with a speaker or other participant to gain their insights and equally important, to exchange referrals and other support. A number of participants have subsequently asked me to speak at their association meetings and referred clients to me.

Planning and hosting a conference can be time consuming, but if done correctly it can help strengthen your reputation as the expert in your field and significantly enhance your database.

ABOUT ED

Ed Craine is a nationally recognized expert in commercial and residential real estate financing.

He is the CEO of award-winning Smith Craine Real Estate Financing in San Francisco.

Ed and his company have won numerous awards for excellence, including being named California Mortgage Broker of the Year 2008 and one of the 10 Leading Mortgage Broker Providers of the United States in 2009.

He is a sought after speaker, trainer, and writer on mortgage and real estate topics. He has been interviewed by numerous media sources including major TV and radio affiliates in Los Angeles and San Francisco as well as print and online media including The Wall Street Journal, Money Magazine, the LA Times, and the San Francisco Chronicle. Recently Ed became the publisher of a leading Mortgage industry trade publication.

Ed is active in industry trade associations, where he has held a variety of executive and board positions. He is currently the President of the California Association of Mortgage Professionals.

Ed is also widely known for his business networking expertise. He is the Executive Director for BNI (Business Network International) in San Francisco, a position he has held since 1997. During this time, he has helped several thousand businesspeople grow their businesses through structured business referral systems.

Ed has won numerous awards, written dozens of articles, and has been a contributing author to three national best-selling business books on sales and networking.

To find out more about using conferences to grow your business, contact Ed at: ed@smithcraine.com or 415-406-2330.

CHAPTER 3

BE THE GIANT AT A NETWORKING EVENT... AFTER THE EVENT!

BY TONY WOLFE

A business associate asked me to attend a networking event with him a while back. I said I would love to. Once I began to ask him a few questions about the event, like who was going to be there and what his goals were while there, I began to realize that he needed some help. I asked him, "What do you want to accomplish when you get there?" Followed by, "Who are you looking to meet?"

How many times have you attended a networking event only to walk away saying to yourself, "WOW! What a complete waste of time that was!" Unfortunately, it happens quite frequently. It can, however, be easily prevented with some proper prior planning and a focus on building strategic relationships with many of the other people who attended the event.

All networking events, whether it is a chamber event, an association or organization mixer or even if you are a member of a regular networking group, should be approached with a strategy and a workable plan that you create ahead of time, and implement at the very beginning of acknowledging that you are attending. Your planning before the event can make you a GIANT after the event.

So, you schedule yourself to attend a networking event that is taking place a few weeks from today. What now? Do you just wait for the date to get here so you can go and "network" with people? No. You do some preplanning now so you will be prepared to be successful when you walk in the door. Because you have planned and strategized ahead of time, you walk into the room with a visible level of confidence. This is a credibility builder. When people see you as confident, they tend to associate that with successful. Successful people like being around other successful people. Who better to build a relationship with than other successful business professionals?

As we are growing our business and building our relationships, we should carry ourselves and project the image that we are already successful and have the confidence that will attract others. You may already have success and that is wonderful, congratulations! For those of you that are still working hard to get there, this will be of great help to you.

For those of you who are allergic to work, I don't know what to tell you other than I hope that works out for you (…said with a smile). For those of you are willing to roll up your sleeves and realize that nothing comes easy, you and I can celebrate together after you apply this process to your regular regimen of successful business networking.

Building your ultimate network begins first with identifying what that network actually looks like. Who would populate it? Consider the strategy of building an all-star team to make up a powerful network that would surround you. Remember also that not only are these all-stars in your network, but you are also in theirs. You must be able to produce and provide for them as well. In fact, that should be your focus. We will talk about that a little later.

With whom do you need to align yourself in order to create a relationship that is mutually beneficial? Will you be able to give them enough that they will want to keep associating with you? Do you plan to just take, take, take and not give, give, give? I can assure you right now, that an 'all-take and no-give' plan will not provide you with the desired results. It just won't. So don't even waste your time with that nonsense.

In the course of identifying your all-star team, you have an unlimited amount of resources that will help you find these professionals. There is the Internet, your local public library, newspapers and trade publications, as well as, now get this, your current network! Yes, the people who are in your network now can help you build your network. All you have to do is ask them.

As you are planning to attend the networking event, think about who else will be attending and do some research. If you have access to know specifically who will be attending, try to find out as much as you can about the people to whom you would like to be introduced, and come prepared to ask questions about that information. You will be letting them know – based on your questions – that you already know a lot about them, and in a very non-stalker sort of way, you want to know more.

Let's say you do not have access to knowing exactly who is in the room. That's what onsite Ambassadors and Connectors are there for. These are people within the organization or group who can introduce you to the specific people that you want to talk to. They know who is in the room. They are established members of the organization, and their role is to connect attendees so that these relationships can begin and grow. It makes the organization successful also. Even when you do know exactly who you want to meet, these Ambassadors and Connectors are the people who can make the introduction happen.

You may also opt for an introduction by a fellow member who you know, who already has credibility with that business professional. That is another great way to get established with that potential contact, because you are trusted by the person who is introducing you. It moves you closer to being credible faster.

Now you are in the room, and you have been introduced to one of your hopefuls. The discussion that you have is very important. If you know enough about this individual to be able to ask more questions relating to their business, that will clue them in on the fact that you have done your homework, you might just be climbing up that ladder even faster as a result.

Engaging them in this conversation and making it all about them is important. Too many people at networking events try to meet as many people as they can, and get their business card in the hands of as many people as possible. They try to make it all about themselves. They try to push their cards and sell their product or service when they first meet people. That is simply not effective networking. If your goal is to attract someone toward having a business relationship with you, you must remember it will take time to get there.

If you are truly interested in connecting and staying in touch in an effort to build a relationship with them, ask for their card. Tell them that you would like to stay in touch. *Here is the part that may be difficult to swallow. If they don't ask for your card, then they don't get your card.* Not right now anyway. Avoid pushing it into their hand. You can include it with your follow up thank you note mentioned below. Chances are, if you have respected their time and kept the conversation about them and proven that you are interested in helping them, they will ask for your card because they have begun to like you.

Now that you have done your homework, researched your prospects, been introduced and had your first conversation with them, now what? If you have done everything right up to now, you have left them with a great first impression. That is one of the keys to this process. What you do from this point on is absolutely critical.

You are still building a foundation on which, potentially for many years to come, you will build a more solid relationship. Remember earlier when I mentioned that you are building a mutually beneficial professional relationship? Well, now is your chance to continue the giving. Keep giving and giving and then give some more. This giving will come back to you in multiples.

Start with a simple, handwritten thank you card. Let them know you enjoyed meeting them and that you look forward to learning more about how you can help them. Again, make it all about them. They will get your card, smile and remember you. Find out who they are trying to connect with and work hard to make those connections for them. You are creating value in yourself and they will automatically want to give back to you.

As you are helping your new business contact(s) with their issues, concerns, wants and desires, you are gaining trust, credibility and they will just generally like you, which means they will be going the extra mile to continue to help you. This process just keeps growing and growing, and has huge rewards for everyone involved.

Learn the skills, products and services of all of your contacts so that you can refer them to one another and others. People really like other people who have solutions to their problems. They find value in resourceful connections. As you learn more about them, you can help them more.

Nurturing the relationship is key. Out of sight, out of mind is 'alive and well.' You must stay front and center with your network. If you lose touch, someone else will swoop in and then you will be left out in the cold.

Here is a five step plan for your next (and every) networking event:

1. Plan Ahead: Set goals before you arrive, so you know exactly what you want to accomplish when you get there.
2. Use Available Resources: Remember to utilize event ambassadors and connectors at the event. That's why they are there! Have them introduce you to the key people that you would like to meet.
3. Make It All About Them: Keep the conversation on them. Once they recognize that you have a genuine interest in helping them, you will build credibility with them. If they ask about you, answer their questions.
4. Follow Up: This is absolutely crucial. Send that hand-written note. Make the phone call. Stay in touch with them. It's why you wanted to talk with them in the first place, to stay connected to them.
5. Nurture the Relationship: Just like you would nurture the relationships of your marriage, your closest friend and your family members, you must also maintain the relationships of your network.

My business associate that I mentioned at the beginning of this chapter has implemented this process. He and I attend events together and he works that room! He has been thrilled with the results.

Everybody knows that business is about relationships. People will buy from those that they know, like and trust. Getting known, being likable and getting to the point of being trusted takes work, patience, persistence and most importantly, time. Your "target" may not respond right away because they are being cautious. That is normal. You would be too. Take the time to prove yourself. There is no rush. Do it right the first time and you can avoid having to repair any damage.

As you can see, being the GIANT after the event takes a lot of activity before and during as well as afterwards. When you begin to focus on building these quality relationships with key people to build your network, in time, you will begin to experience amazing results in the quality of your networking efforts and the relationships that you build.

ABOUT TONY

Tony Wolfe is a professional voice actor, on-camera talent, MC, speaker/presenter, best-selling author and has been heard around the globe. With his motivating *GO DO!*™ attitude, he will surely bring a positive and productive result to any project or event. Known as "The Man Of A Thousand Voices…Give or Take a Few," he began his voice-acting career performing characters and impersonations for a morning drive-time radio show. This afforded him fourteen well-invested years of experience where he developed characters, wrote and performed in comedy bits, and provided voiceovers for commercials and imaging projects. He even made comedy stage appearances as some of the characters he portrayed on the show.

Some of Tony's projects include: an animated children's program where he provided voices for eight of the fifteen characters in the pilot. He is the voice of Fischers Meats' "Mr. Bologna" and his Jimmy Stewart impersonation has been used as a promo for NBC's TODAY Show. He is also the voice of The Redneck Horn, which was featured on The Tonight Show with Jay Leno as one of the best novelty Christmas gifts, which later became the second best-selling novelty item in Spencer Gifts stores nationwide.

Tony also provides more serious reads for a wide variety of projects. For example, he was in the emergency services arena from 1986 to 2006 as a firefighter/medic and a medicolegal death investigator from 1989 to 2009. His voice adds a level of knowledge and sincerity for projects in the medical and law enforcement related fields. Tony is listed in several talent pools, and his voice is used for projects in numerous studios all over the United States, Canada and Australia. Whether it is on-hold messages, online college courses, training videos, podcasts, audio books or characters for any application, Tony is always eagerly seeking new opportunities to expand and diversify his talent portfolio.

Tony is a contributing author to the best-selling book *The World's Worst Networker – Lessons Learned by the Best From the Absolute Worst.*

He is also the owner of Paradyme Marketing and is an Assistant Director for BNI (Business Network International) in Central Kentucky and Southern Indiana. **Contact:** Email: tw@tonywolfe.com or call (812) 945-8669.

CHAPTER 4

THE MAGIC OF CATALYST EVENTS

BY STEVE HAND

From a little spark may burst a flame.
~ Dante Alighieri

O nce upon a time there was a new Financial Planner who quickly built his business with only thirty-two clients. Naturally, in order to make this successful, these had to be very high net-worth individuals. Because, he reasoned, with only a few customers he would have the time needed to provide each one with all the care and attention required for their mutual benefit. **He built that practice in less than eighteen months by leveraging the magic of catalyst events.** So, too, can you.

Does that get your attention? Have you been working to build your business in the many traditional ways with limited success? Have you tried catalyst events? Do you even know what they are?

Although professionals have used catalyst events for thousands of years, most business people are only dimly aware of them, if at all.

Think of the many different types of <u>events</u> along a scale where the "sales quotient" goes from almost non-existent to very high. At the **high end** is the pressure cooker sales experience of attending a time-share presentation, walking onto an automotive showroom floor, or attending a network marketing opportunity meeting in a hotel. Makes you shudder a bit, doesn't it? At the **low end** would be a child's birthday party, a wedding, or other family-based events.

If we think of that scale as a speedometer from zero to sixty, from low or no sales to boiler room pressure, then catalyst events are at about six or seven miles per hour. It might be even lower than that and certainly not much higher.

People look forward to them. They come to enjoy themselves.

Let's consider one of the early masters of the catalyst event. Elmer Letterman was one of the most successful insurance salesmen in the world working in the late nineteen-twenties. He used these events exclusively. In fact, exclusivity was one of the keys to his success. Mr. Letterman arranged lunch every day—Monday through Friday—with three other people at the *Four Seasons Hotel* in Manhattan. This was a very high-end restaurant and he was not there to talk about insurance. If anyone asked about that, his response was simply, "My associate will call you." Mr. Letterman became extremely successful.

Our Financial Planner followed a similar formula in pursuit of his thirty-two clients and the good news is that you can, too. Before going too far, though, we need to make sure our terminology is clear.

The *American Heritage Dictionary* has two definitions for the noun "catalyst." First, from chemistry, a catalyst is a substance, typically used in small amounts relative to the reactants, that modifies and increases the rate of a reaction without being consumed in the process. Although that's challenging language, it is worth pondering a moment.

A catalyst is also something (or someone) that causes a process or event, especially without being involved in or changed by the consequences, e.g., "A free press ... has remained ... a vital catalyst to an informed and responsible electorate" (Robert O'Neal).

Additionally, there are a few criteria that make a catalyst event what it is. We mentioned **low pressure** and that is one hallmark. These are relationship-building exercises. Selling is never allowed and never tolerated.

It is also important to have a **servant's heart**. Be there to help. Host rather than guest, and facilitate wherever possible.

Let's look a little closer, though, at a few other key points:

The first is that the event must be **special**. That is, not something most people would ordinarily do. Mr. Letterman knew that most people would not spring for lunch at the *Four Seasons Hotel*. This made the invitation itself a special event. He usually arranged them a few weeks in advance.

In your own world there is a wide range of events that can meet this. Pick something you enjoy, as well. In the outdoor world that might be hang-gliding, hot-air-ballooning, sailing, horseback riding, golf, and so on. The more exotic (or exclusive) the better. In the indoor arena you have sporting events, theater, music, art, dance, cooking and so on. These events can be participatory or observational, although **participation usually heightens the experience**.

The event should also be **suitable for everyone** involved. Some like opera, …some do not!

Whatever you select, make it **memorable** in some way. If you like opera, then arrange to attend the cast party on opening night, for example.

Catalyst events should also always address the key questions journalists consider in any story. Specifically, these are who, what, where, when, and why.

With that in mind, let's return to our Financial Planner and the magic of catalyst events.

He selected trout fishing as the experience. The primary reason was that he enjoyed the sport and wanted to share it with others. The secondary reason was that Robert Redford's movie *A River Runs Through It* was current in movie theaters.

This took care of the **what** and the **why**.

He selected a date a few weeks out to take care of the **when**.

He already knew his favorite trout stream, about ninety minutes away, and that was the **where**.

This only left the **who**, which, incidentally, may be the most important consideration of all. It certainly was for Mr. Letterman. He arranged his daily luncheons around 'who' the other person wanted to meet. Let's say that his best friend, Joe Smith, is in the shipping business and would like to meet the mayor. Mr. Letterman was reasonably well-connected and knew (or knew someone who knew) the mayor. He would call the politician and find out when he was available and who *he* would like to meet. Perhaps it might be a starlet from the hot new show on Broadway. Mr. Letterman arranged for all three of these people to have lunch together with him. Naturally, the logistics of making this happen every day took many phone calls and impromptu visits. He owed favors and cashed favors along the way. As his guest list grew, so did his reputation and the legend of these lunches. Coincidentally, his current namesake, David Letterman, does a similar thing on late night television.

Hasten slowly

~ Augustus

Our Financial Planner wanted to fish with millionaires. Now, you can certainly change that adverb to fish "for" millionaires, but the bottom line is no selling allowed. *Building relationships is the key objective.* Even if none of his new fishing buddies become clients, they will all have a good time. Naturally, millionaires know other millionaires, but the event must stand on its own for its own sake.

He discussed his planned event with the local tackle shop in order to arrange to rent equipment and secure a fishing guide to teach these neophytes the basics. The astute fishing gear owner was tickled with the opportunity to work with millionaires as well, and arranged for a special shop tour and training – the morning of the trip. In addition, the fishing guide would be included for free.

The next call was to arrange transportation. He felt *Land Rovers* would be an appropriate vehicle in keeping with the spirit of the event. A friend of a friend knew the local *Land Rover* dealer. When this gentleman heard about the idea, he offered him all the vehicles he needed for free as long his best salesman could accompany them all.

With these and other logistics coming together, he started to invite his guests. This would be a good chance to meet other people and have a memorable time fishing in a very exclusive stream. Guests were encouraged to bring guests.

The morning arrived and the weather was perfect. They met at the tackle store and enjoyed coffee and breakfast biscuits, courtesy of a local caterer. Together, they toured the facility, tied a simple fly together, and took their first lesson in the parking lot. Picture fifteen wealthy gentlemen waving their fly rods in the predawn darkness and you can imagine the scene. Since the Financial Planner had fished all his life, he was able to help many of them. There's that servant's heart in action.

After that, they drove through the mountains to the stream and spent some quality time getting to know one another. This was an interesting crowd of movers and shakers. None were shy. All were glad to share their stories with new peers.

This fishing was excellent. Again, our Financial Planner was more attentive to the needs of the guests. As much as he loved casting, this was not a day for him to fish.

Our Financial Planner arranged for lunch—brought in by the same caterer—delivered up the mountain to a very hungry crowd. The guide helped them clean the few fish they kept. These were cooked on the riverbank.

Before the day was done, everyone already looked forward to the next event. Since it was such a success, our Financial Planner chose another date—about a month away—and continued that pace through the rest of the season.

He personally went fishing on the in-between weekends with one or two people at a time. The group fishing trips are now just annual events—usually to more exotic locations and his practice is thriving.

These events do not have to be elaborate, however.

One of the most successful residential Realtors in our area hosts an annual catalyst event. Along with his wife, this is his twenty-third year serving frittatas in his home on Easter morning. This is simple and effective.

I have been an entrepreneur all my life—starting with a paper route. We delivered the afternoon papers and a Sunday morning edition, as well. Most of my fellow paperboys hated Sundays, so they paid me to handle their Sunday routes. I took the funds, rounded up all my friends to deliver the papers, and popped for a big communal breakfast or early morning ball game or whatever we had planned for that week. In time, I had a waiting list of delivery people and made more money on Sunday than any other day of the week.

As a very young man, I had a different target audience in mind. My friend and I wanted to meet girls. He had a lot of musical talent and business skills while I had a small amount of each. We put our heads together and decided to start an advertising business. With the catchy name of *Radio and Television Advertising* we were off to the marketplace. At our age, we were exactly the demographic all the New York City media wanted to capture. They wined and dined us aggressively, which was a lot of fun (and good for dating scenarios, as well.)

We signed up some restaurants, pet stores, banks, car repair places…a bowling alley. It was fun to hear the jingles we wrote and sang on the radio. It was also fun to film those silly commercials we did in the *Monty Python* style. We designed a few logos and brochures.

The key events, though, were our casting parties. This is, in fact, where I met the woman of my dreams who became my bride thirty years ago. Consider catalyst events in your business and all your dreams may come true, too.

Just as energy is the basis of life itself, and ideas the source of innovation, so is innovation the vital spark of all human change, improvement and progress. ~ Ted Levitt

ABOUT STEVE

Always bear in mind that your own resolution to succeed is more important than any one thing. ~ Abraham Lincoln

Steve Hand is an Executive Director of *Business Network International*. BNI is the world's leader in word-of-mouth marketing, with more than 125,000 members in forty countries. Last year BNI members passed roughly 6.2 million referrals, generating more than $2.6 billion (USD) worth of business for their members globally.

Steve is a passionate teacher and ambassador for the power of referral-based sales, and is looking forward to helping take your networking skills to new heights. He has been an entrepreneur from a very early age, buying his first car at age 11. To be more precise, he was a 20% owner of a little *Hillman Minx*. "None of us were old enough to drive on the street but we ran that little car hard up and down the driveway all day long. It didn't take long to start renting rides and we ultimately made a handsome profit before the summer was out."

Steve has a strong background in technology services and has been self-employed since 1997. In addition to helping nearly 700 clients enjoy $15 million in profits annually, Steve teaches beginner poker and the *Cashflow* board game.

His wife, Shirley, teaches at the *Governor Morehead School for the Blind* and co-published *Seeing Beyond Sight*, a book about photography classes for blind students that was well received by the *New York Times*.

Steve's personal goal is to drive passive income above active expenses.

You can learn more about the Triangle region of *Business Network International* at: www.trianglebni.com, follow his weekly blog at: http://bniguy.wordpress.com/, or call toll-free at 1-877-500-0842.

CHAPTER 5

10 LEVELS OF REFERRALS

BY DR. IVAN MISNER

The more involvement from the referral source in securing the referral, the stronger the opportunity to close the sale.

A referral is a referral, right? Once a referral source has given you the name of a person to call, it's up to you to do the rest. A referral is better than a cold call because you have the name of the prospect, and, if you're fortunate, you can use the name of the referral source to open the door. What more could you hope for?

Actually, there's quite a bit more you can expect from referrals that have been properly developed by their sources.

Referrals come in many different grades. I've identified ten levels of referrals that vary in quality according to how much involvement your referral source has invested in preparing the referral for you. The more time and effort your source puts into qualifying, educating, and encouraging the prospect before you become involved, the higher the quality and level of that referral. Conversely, if your referral source only passes a prospect's name to you, most of the work of converting that prospect into a customer falls on you, and the likelihood diminishes significantly.

Of course, the effectiveness of your referral network in providing you with quality referrals depends on the amount of work you do to develop your sources. There are many ways to encourage them to become active and enthusiastic members of your marketing team. In this chapter, we'll address several methods for building the effectiveness of your referral network. The Networking Scorecard (explained in the next chapter) will enable you to track the work you are doing to develop your network. By using this scorecard to keep a weekly record of your network development efforts and the quality of referrals you receive, you'll begin to see the relationship between two.

Now let's cover the ten levels of referrals, ranging from "nothing but name" to "the full Monty." I ranked them in order of ascending quality.

LEVEL 1.
NAMES AND CONTACT INFORMATION ONLY

This isn't much better than having just a name to call. It only indicates that your referral source has done just enough work to provide you with a phone number, address, or some other way of contacting the prospect.

LEVEL 2.
LITERATURE, BIOGRAPHY, AND COMPANY INFORMATION

When a referral source offers to give a contact your marketing literature or other information about your business, all you can be certain of is that the prospect will see the materials. The prospect's interest in your product or service will depend solely on the impact of your marketing message.

LEVEL 3.
AUTHORIZATION TO USE NAME

Once a referral source has authorized you to use her name, you can feel fairly certain that you've established a good level of credibility with her. By allowing you to say that she endorses your product or service, your source has given you valuable leverage with the prospect; however, the problem with this shade of referral is that the burden of developing the prospect still rests on you. Once you've conveyed that your referral source recommends you and your business, the task of selling really begins.

LEVEL 4.
GENERAL TESTIMONIAL OR LETTER OF RECOMMENDATION

Getting a referral source to say or write nice things about you is a major accomplishment. His willingness to communicate positively about you and your business shows that you've built a moderate level of trust with him. Of course, testimonials and letters of recommendation are fairly common in the business world, so their impact on the average person is limited.

LEVEL 5.
LETTER OF INTRODUCTION AND PROMOTION

This is the first level of referral that truly involves a modicum of effort on the part of your referral source. Unlike the letter of recommendation, which requires little more than a written endorsement, the note or letter of introduction implies a more substantive relationship between you and the referral source, and it usually includes background information and a description of your product or service as filtered through the lens of the author. It also infers that the prospect will be hearing from you.

Adding the element of promotion increases the effectiveness of your referral source's effort on your behalf. Promotion is advocacy—an outright recommendation of your product or service with a description of its features and benefits.

LEVEL 6.
INTRODUCTION CALL AND PROMOTION

Another level up in terms of effort is the referral source that makes a personal phone call on your behalf. It takes preparation and effort, but a telephone call from your source is more effective than a letter for paving your way to communicate with the prospect. Including a promotion makes it even more favorable.

LEVEL 7.
ARRANGING A MEETING

Your referral source moves beyond the role of a promoter to that of a facilitator, taking the responsibility of working out the details of getting you and the prospect together. This is a big-time referral effort.

LEVEL 8.
IN-PERSON INTRODUCTION AND PROMOTION

At this level, your referral source is making a serious commitment of time and energy in support of your business. By agreeing to serve as an intermediary in a face-to-face introduction, your source becomes an active business agent. This demonstration of deep trust in, and approval of your product or service, substantially raises the referral's effectiveness with the prospect. Adding promotion further enhances its power, because your source is then actively engaged in selling your product or service rather than just facilitating a meeting.

LEVEL 9.
ASSESSING NEED AND INTEREST

For this level of referrals, your referral source has done the work of assessing the need a prospect may have for your product or service, and has gauged the prospect's interest in learning more about it. This enables you to focus your selling effort to needs you know the prospect has an intention to fill, and it allows you to select or tailor your products or services to provide specific benefits.

LEVEL 10.
CLOSED DEAL

At the top level of referrals, the sale has been closed before you even contact the prospect, solely on the strength of your referral source's efforts. Nothing else is required from you except to deliver the product or service and collect payment.

The amount of work you have to do to close a deal is based on the level of the referral. If you're given a Level 1 referral, you have to do 95 percent of the work to close; this is not much better than a cold call. On the other hand, if you get a Level 9 or 10 referral, then the person giving you the referral has already done most of the work for you. It's easier for your referral source to close the deal than it is for you, because your source already has a relationship of trust with your prospect. For this reason, it's important for you to do a superb job in fulfilling that referral – so your referrer will get great feedback and want to refer you again. The referral-giver is, in essence, lending you her credibility; this is not something to be taken lightly.

ABOUT IVAN

Dr. Ivan Misner is the Founder & Chairman of BNI (*www.bni.com*), the world's largest business networking organization. BNI was founded in 1985. The organization now has over 6,000 chapters throughout every populated continent of the world. Last year alone, BNI generated 6.5 million referrals resulting in $2.8 billion dollars worth of business for its members.

Dr. Misner's Ph.D. is from the University of Southern California. He is a *New York Times* Bestselling author who has written over 12 books, including his latest one, called *Networking Like a Pro,* which can be viewed at: *www.IvanMisner.com.* He is a monthly columnist for Entrepreneur.com and is the Senior Partner for the Referral Institute – an international referral training company *(www.referralinstitute.com),* with trainers around the world. In addition, he has taught business management and social capital courses at several universities throughout the United States.

Called the *"Father of Modern Networking"* by CNN and the *"Networking Guru"* by Entrepreneur magazine, Dr. Misner is considered to be one of the world's leading experts on business networking, and has been a keynote speaker for major corporations and associations throughout the world. He has been featured in *The L.A. Times, The Wall Street Journal,* and *The New York Times,* as well as numerous TV and radio shows, including *CNN, CNBC,* and the *BBC* in London.

Dr. Misner is on the Board of Trustees for the University of LaVerne, CA. He is also the Founder of the BNI-Misner Charitable Foundation and was recently named *"Humanitarian of the Year"* by a Southern California newspaper.

He is married and lives with his wife Elisabeth and their three children in Claremont, CA. *In his spare time(!!!),* he is also an amateur magician and has a black belt in karate.

CHAPTER 6

THE ASSOCIATIONS ASSOCIATE

BY NICHOLAS J. ZOLFO

I n the mid-1990's I ventured out to start my own business, and was trying everything to obtain clients. This is when I first heard the term "Networking." The funny thing was that with all the business courses I had taken in college, there was no mention of the term. I had very limited funds for advertising and the constant rejection from cold calling was taking an emotional toll.

Being in my twenties, having only a handful of clients, I was hungry and eager to learn about the real business world. What they did not teach me in college and this concept of networking was on the top of my list. I began reading everything I could find on the topic of networking (which in 1997 was very little compared to today). I realized that I needed to meet with other business professionals, with whom I could build face-to-face relationships – with the hopes of growing my business.

I became a member of my local trade association for my field, and began attending seminars to obtain credits in order to keep my industry license in good standing. The seminars were filled with people in my industry. Basically, they were my competitors. At the largest seminar of the year, the association also sponsored a trade show with vendors that supplied products and services to my industry. It turned out that these vendors were also members of the association. They were known as "Associate Members." There are many privileges to which an "Associate Member" is entitled. Some of these may include being allowed to join committees, attend events, being listed in a certain section of the member directory and website sponsorship.

I found this concept to be very intriguing. The clients I was looking to obtain were commercial and corporate accounts, and thought if I could get into other associations in this capacity, it would put me in direct contact with the decision-makers that I was trying to attract through advertising and cold calling. The main obstacle I faced was to find the associations that I needed to get involved with. I decided to take a close look at my client list to see which industries I wanted to increase my presence in. I then met with a client in that industry and inquired about the association they belonged to for their profession and requested the contact information. They gladly obliged, and shortly after, I was an "Associate Member" of that association.

After attending a few of their meetings and making my presence known, one of the members actually approached me and asked me to contact him in order to present a proposal for service. Within a week, I had a new client. Here's the punch line, I knew of this person. He practically hung up on me when I cold-called him two months earlier. I'm sure he had no recollection of that call, since he probably receives cold calls all day long. If not for networking through this association as an "Associate Member," this new client would never have become reality.

If you are looking to grow your business through Networking, one avenue you need to try is getting involved with trade organizations where the members are the type of clients you want to attract. Depending on the association, there are different terms for the "Associate Member" status. Some of the other terms are "Vendor Member," "Allied Member" and "Affiliate Member."

Applying for membership in an association and paying the required dues alone will not let you reap the rewards of joining. It is what you do with your membership that will make the difference. Let's explore some steps you can take to make the most of your "Associate" status and become the "Associations Associate."

STEP #1:
FORMULATE A PLAN

a.. You cannot effectively grow your business through networking if you have a cavalier attitude or 'try to wing it.' You need to create a sound plan for how you will approach this avenue of growing your business.

b. When getting involved with an association, you will need to invest time and money. Begin by calculating the length of time on average your company retains a new client. Over the lifetime of that client, how much revenue will they generate for your company? How much are the membership dues for the association? What are the fees for their events and tradeshows that you will want to attend? How much time will you have to dedicate to meetings and building relationships with the other members?

c. You will need to sit down and write out the above questions and answers. This will help you understand how many new clients you will need to obtain over the course of a year to make your return on investment worthwhile.

d. Write down specific goals you wish to achieve through the association. Next, write down the methods you will need to follow to achieve those goals. If you do not set goals, you will never accomplish them.

e. Track your results! Setting goals is only the beginning. You must periodically track your results. This will allow you to evaluate which methods are working and which methods need to be fine-tuned. Achieving success through networking in an association does not happen over-night. This will take time, and tracking your results will allow you the opportunity to improve your approach and skills.

STEP #2:
FIND THE RIGHT ASSOCIATION

a. There are associations for most professions and some industries have several. You need to sit back and decide what type of clients you want to attract. What is your geographic area? What markets do you want to create a presence in?

b. Choose an association that will put you in direct contact with the decision makers of those markets. You may want to start with an association that is geared towards an industry where you have some established clients and want to expand that specific client base. By doing this, you will already have references to present to prospects that you meet through the association. People prefer to use those that have experience providing products/services to their industry.

c. Associations can also be local, regional or national. Depending on the geographic location of your client base and/or territory will help simplify your choices. Remember that you need to get involved with an association where you can physically participate in their meeting and events.

d. I feel the easiest way to find out the name of an association is to speak to current clients. Find out what associations they are involved with and if they allow associate type members. Look on their walls. There is a good chance that a member plaque from the association will be displayed. This is a great ice breaker to have a conversation about the association. "Excuse me, Ms. Smith; I noticed the plaque on the wall. Could you tell me a little about the _____ association?" Also, the power of the Internet makes locating associations very simple. With many associations, you can either apply online, download an application to send in, or send a request to receive information on membership. Some associations will require an associate member to be sponsored by a full member. If you speak to your clients that you have a quality relationship with, they should have no problem sponsoring you into the association.

STEP #3:
SOMETIMES LESS IS MORE

a. In the beginning, apply for membership in the one association that you have decided would be a good fit for your company. Don't over extend yourself by joining several associations right 'out of the starting gate.' You need to remember that you will need to devote time to the association. If you get involved in too many associations right away, you will not be able to dedicate the proper amount of time, and you will be spreading yourself too thin.

b. In order to benefit from an association, you will need to work the association. Sounds simple enough. However, this will require a certain level of commitment. You will need to get involved and participate in the association in order to build the proper level of trust with the members. This will allow you the opportunity to present your business to them. Having your information listed in a member directory alone will not create the relationships required for others to want to do business with you.

STEP #4:
GET INVOLVED

a. Attend events and don't be a wall flower. Associations have regular meetings and events. You will be the new kid on the block and also the one looking to meet potential clients. It is your responsibility to introduce yourself to those in attendance. You are looking to make contacts and get to know people. It is up to you to initiate and nurture the relationship.

b. Do not push to sell your product/service. The members will learn through general conversation what line of business you are in. Build the relationship first, present your business second. The members are quite aware of why you became a member. Learn about them and then you can express how you and your business can help them. Nobody likes to be made to feel as if the other person is just looking to make a quick buck at their expense.

c. During your membership in an association, there will be opportunities to get involved in a committee and/or helping out with an event – charity, social or otherwise. Volunteer when the occasion presents itself. It will elevate your reputation within the organization. You will also be working side-by-side with the members you want to approach as prospects. You will want to budget for "give-ways" with your company logo on them for events where the association needs members to donate door prizes and / or items for a goodie bag.

STEP #5:
EVERYONE IS A POTENTIAL CLIENT

a. At times, we will prejudge someone before knowing all the facts. This is the same in business. You may think: "They will never use my product / service." "They cannot afford what I have to offer." "They don't know the people I want to be introduced to."

b. Sometimes your best clients can come from the most unlikely sources. You never know who other people know. Your initial intention for getting involved in an association as an associate member is to get in front of the decision makers of your target market. However, don't disregard the other associate members. Especially those that are not your competitors. Clearly they are part of the association because they too deal with the same type of clients that you do. Network with them as well. Building relationships with the other associate members will open doors to additional prospects outside the circle of the association. Become referral partners with other associate members.

c. Give back! Networking is not for the selfish. To be successful in networking you need to embrace the philosophy *to give without expecting something in return*. If you do, you will receive.

STEP #6:
FOLLOW-UP

a. You may be thinking that this is common sense. Yet sometimes the simplest tasks are the ones we often overlook.

b. You need to follow-up with those you meet in the association. Follow-up on a regular basis. I prefer a personal touch. A quick phone call to say hello or a hand written card. Whichever methods you decide to use, you must do them consistently. You are the one looking to grow your business, so it is up to you to nurture the relationship.

c. During association events, the members will be spending time with your competitors. This is an obstacle you will need to overcome in order to get the members to truly know you and your business. Set yourself above the rest. Follow-up! Follow-up! Follow-up!

ABOUT NICHOLAS

Nicholas J Zolfo, "Nick" to most, was born and raised in New York City. The son of career salespeople, Nick began his sales career at an early age. He worked selling candy to the neighborhood kids from the wagon attached to his bicycle at the age of seven, to selling cutlery door-to-door while in his teens. Nick knew then that in one form or another, he would always be in the business of sales. A graduate of St. John's University, Nick obtained his degree in communications and business in 1992. After spending some years in the corporate sales world, Nick ventured out to start his own business. There were two certainties that Nick quickly understood: First, he needed to generate sales to grow his business. Second, he was not a fan of the "old-school–hard-sales" mentality that he was exposed to throughout his youth.

While building his business, Nick found a passion for Networking. He began studying the topic and applying the techniques to a variety of aspects of his life. He also became involved in different organizations, like Industry Associations, the local Chamber of Commerce and especially BNI. BNI is the largest one-person professional networking organization in the world.

For over nine years, Nick has been involved in the BNI organization. He started off as a chapter member and then became an area director in New Jersey. One of Nick's responsibilities as an area director is training and mentoring other business professionals on the art of networking. Nick is also involved in the development and presentation of business seminars.

Nick is now sharing his knowledge and experiences through the written word by embarking as an author with his first venture as a contributing author for the book ~ *Building the Ultimate Network.*

CHAPTER 7

NEVER TREAT YOUR NETWORK EQUALLY

BY MARK M. DEUTSCH, MBA

Have you ever felt like a hamster in a wheel? A networking wheel at least. Running yourself ragged attending every networking event possible, making hundreds of new contacts... but none of them ever pan out and your revenue isn't growing at the pace you would like. It's okay. You are not alone and help is here. I have been there, done that, and I got the t-shirt.

As a freshly-minted sales representative for a mid-sized, young health-care company just out of college and ready to tackle the world, I was trained to do just that – go to a city, grab a phone book, and start making calls (this was pre-internet by the way — so be sure to Google "phone book" or go to a Museum of Modern History to see one). I joined every organization imaginable, the local Chambers of Commerce, the local physician associations, Toastmasters. I also exhibited at trade shows, advertised in medical journals, etcetera, etcetera. You know the drill. I gathered thousands of business cards in my first year, and subsequently threw them away at the end of my first year. They were getting me nowhere, there had to be a better way.

It was then that I received some sage business advice (and about life, for that matter) from a very successful business owner who took me under his wing after I shared my frustrations with him: You should never treat people equally, but you should always treat them fairly. I have applied this philosophy throughout the course of my 25-year-plus career to build an unparalleled personal and professional network. Contrary to the popular thought in today's wired world of having a massive list of prospects, or just adding everyone you meet to your e-newsletter list, you can build a referral fortress that couldn't even be penetrated by the Huns, if you treat the members of your network fairly.

I see it in training business owners, entrepreneurs, and sales people every day – they know that referral and word-of-mouth marketing are the best ways to do business, so they attend dozens of business and social networking events every month. They accumulate many opportunities that lie in stacks of 3½ x 2 inch 'fields of dreams,' but they fail to convert them to reality. This is due largely, if not entirely, to the flawed thought that you can and should stay in touch with every single person you meet versus building a deep relationship with a select few. In the business world, where we are so often told that "sales is a numbers game," master networkers know that the opposite is actually the truth – depth trumps width. The challenge is implementing a system that allows you to most effectively treat the members of your networks as they deserve to be treated.

It's a lot like the process of finding a spouse. One strategy is to simply go to a bar and just ask every person there if they'd like to marry you. Statistics tell us that at some point, after you endure enough slaps to your face, someone will say yes (Sounds a lot like cold calling, doesn't it?). Another strategy is to build deep, productive relationships with a few people who genuinely know, like, trust, and respect you – and they will work to find a great mate for you (that's how I found mine, a blind date I was set-up with that worked out!). I have developed a simple system to do just that, investing your time and energy in people that matter. I call it the "Relationship Cultivation System" or "RCS" to save some ink. Here are the three steps to the RCS:

1. Compile
2. Categorize
3. Cultivate

STEP NUMBER 1:
COMPILE YOUR DATABASE.

If you haven't done so already, it's time to take those thousands of business cards and get them in to an electronic database. If you don't have a well-maintained database of your networks, meaning everyone you have ever met in your life if possible, you will fail. Yes, that is a bold statement, but it is unequivocally true. Ask any billionaire if they disagree with this fact. You don't need an especially fancy database to achieve this step, and I've used them all - ACT!, Goldmine, Salesforce. com, iContact, Constant Contact, Zoho, and InfusionSoft to name a few. My preference now is simple – Microsoft Outlook. I use it every day for email anyway, and it is easy to customize for my needs. It works for me. The bottom line is to do what it takes to get those people in there. I chose to outsource this step to a client of mine who was able to scan 95% of the more than 10,000 cards I had handy into a spreadsheet using a card scanner and then I just imported them into Outlook. That got my database started; now I systematically add new contacts manually as I go.

STEP NUMBER 2:
CATEGORIZE YOUR DATABASE.

Now you need to prioritize this priceless database, and I recommend keeping this process simple. I do so because the next step, cultivation, involves determining ways to consistently and effectively communicate with various members of your network. There are hundreds of potential ways to categorize or "segment" your database. For example, here are a few: demographics, psychographics, lifestyle, belief and value systems, life stage, email address vs. no email address, interest-based preferences, title, referred by, source, clicked links, recency, networking event, frequency, money spent, product/service purchased, sales stage, former clients, activity level, and the list goes on. Too complicated, right? I agree, so here's my simple A, B, C, and D system that is time and battle-tested.

- "A's" – clients who have referred you and referral partners who have referred you, or are most likely to refer you based on their profession or ability to do so.

- "B's" – clients or referral partners who would refer you, if taught how.
- "C's" – clients or referral partners who have an outside chance of referring you in the future.
- "D's" – clients or referral partners who you would like to fire! These are the people whose number you see on your caller ID and you sigh, thinking, "Do I actually have to talk to them?" Get these names out of your database, they are wasting valuable resources.

That is it – keep it simple. Realize that most of your database will end up in the "B" and "C" buckets, 80% in fact. 10% will end up in the "A" pile and another 10% in the "D" stack. In my case, I further limit my "A's" to about 200; because that is how many people I can maintain a quality relationship with.

STEP NUMBER 3:
CULTIVATE YOUR DATABASE.

This is the most critical of the three steps to creating and maintaining your RCS, yet I also keep this process simple.

- "A's" – receive a *touch* from me at least monthly.
- "B's" – receive a *touch* from me at least quarterly.
- "C's" – receive a *touch* from me at least yearly.
- "D's" – receive no *touches* other than a 'buh-bye.'

Now allow me to define what I call "touches" – the key to cultivation. A *touch* is where you show appreciation for your clients and referral partners. This appreciation takes the form of a referral for their business if they are a referral partner, a contact (call, e-newsletter, email, text message, etc.), a show of caring (greeting cards and personalized notes, drop-by calls, etc.), or a group event (involving them in a business luncheon/dinner/breakfast/coffee or client appreciation event). It is frankly easier than ever to *touch* your network – poke around social media sites, such as Facebook, LinkedIn, Twitter, and YouTube for what is important to your network – then *touch* them in ways that are meaningful to them.

Similar to the ways in which you can segment your database, there are hundreds of ways you can *touch* or express appreciation to your network members. Here are the top 10 *touches* that I have found to be the most effective:

1. **Greetings cards and personalized notes using the SendOutCards system (www.RelationshipCultivationSystem.com).** Using information or pictures you found in your social media mining efforts, create personalized, hard-copy greeting cards through an on-line service that uses real stamps and mails these high-impact cards through the U.S. Mail. This is an easy, inexpensive, and powerful way to touch your database.

2. **Recognize important dates to your network.** Send birthday cards, anniversary cards (wedding or when they became a client, for example), St. Patrick's Day cards, Hanukah, Chinese New Year and Kwanzaa. Forget sending Christmas cards, send a New Year's card instead – when was the last time someone said, "Thanks for the great Christmas card?"

3. **Watch for events that may be important to your network.** Use your awareness of your network's group affiliations to connect them with the areas of greatest interest to them. For example, if they are active Rotarians, let them know about interesting ways to volunteer in their community.

4. **Pay close attention to announcements about members of your network.** Local newspapers and on-line publications have business sections that feature promotions, new hires, Board appointments, and the like. When a member of your network shows up in one of those columns, don't send a letter or note, pick up the phone and call them. I guarantee that they'll get a number of form letters congratulating them, but they'll remember that you took the time to call them.

5. **A simple email.** A few relevant sentences will do, there's no need to send a long email to people who probably already have way too many emails to read as it is (the average business owner gets over 150 emails a day). Keep it short, sweet, and don't ask for anything; just *touch* them.

6. **Act on your daily prompting.** Make it a daily habit to review your "A" list and pick one at random to call just to see what is new with them.

7. **Don't just pass through without stopping to visit with your**

network members. There may be members of your network in far off lands, especially today. If you are in the area where one of your "A" or "B" players live, take the time to grab a cup of coffee or a beer, take them to lunch or dinner, or call at the very least.

8. **Use Google Alerts.** Go to www.google.com/alerts and sign up for various alerts that pertain to your network members. When you get an alert about them, send them a quick email to let them know that you noticed the news – or even more powerful, make them aware of negative things being said about them.

9. **Send them free stuff.** Everybody loves free stuff. I used to get boxes of two gourmet chocolate truffles from a local chocolatier (less than $1 each) and drop them off to referral sources every time I got a referral from them. This strategy alone has yielded me hundreds of thousands of dollars in business over the years, and it was amazing to see how the referrals would roll in when some folks had a craving for some chocolate!

10. **Be there for them.** Particularly for your "A" team, attend weddings, funerals, award ceremonies, graduations, etc. Believe me, the relationships you develop will last a lifetime.

These are just a few of the ways you can touch your network members in a meaningful way. Regardless of the specific tools you choose, be sure that your Relationship Cultivation System is organized, original, frequent – according to their category, timely, and consistent. In treating every member of your network fairly instead of equally, with respect to your ability to help them and vice versa, you'll discover that your networking is working beyond your wildest dreams. Don't just race to your next networking event only to choke down some stale chicken wings and come home with a pocket full of useless business cards. Take the time to compile, categorize, and cultivate your network, so you can jump off of the treadmill and appreciate your way to success.

ABOUT MARK

Mark M. Deutsch, MBA has been in your shoes. During his 25-year-plus entrepreneurial career, Mark has started or operated more than a dozen companies ranging from a landscaping business (while in middle school) to a medical billing software company (during the dot-com boom). He has been involved at a C-level with businesses that had 0 to 100 employees; start-up to mature stages; with companies that succeeded and others that imploded. After learning some valuable lessons in the school of hard knocks, Mark has determined that your most valuable business asset is your personal and professional network.

Called the "Mayor of Richmond, Virginia," and the "guy who knows everyone," Mark moved to Richmond, VA from Orlando, FL in 1993, knowing no one except the manager of the company he was coming to work for. Today he has a personal and professional network without equal, and Mark is a Master Networker, Author, Speaker, Trainer, Seminar Leader, Online Information Marketer, and life-long Entrepreneur. Currently, Mark is the Executive Director & CEO of BNI (Business Network International) – Central Virginia, the largest and most successful business referral organization in Virginia. He is widely recognized as THE EXPERT for building your business by referrals.

The son of German immigrants who survived forced labor camps after WW II, Mark cut his teeth in an environment of hard work, survival, overcoming obstacles, and bootstrapping. He built his first multi-million dollar company before he was 30 years old, lost it all, and has bounced back. Mark authors hundreds of articles and he speaks more than 200 times every year to trade associations, business organizations, and professional groups on the topics of networking, sales, marketing, search engine marketing, and social media marketing. Mark is an active member of several boards, and he also owns equity positions in a number of small and mid-sized private businesses across a variety of industries. He is a graduate of the University of Central Florida, and received his MBA from Averett University.

To learn more about Mark Deutsch and how you can receive Mark's 75-minute Video – *Increasing Sales in a Sluggish Economy* for free, visit: www.MarkDeutsch.com or call 804-338-3987.

CHAPTER 8

BUILDING SUCCESS WITH THE LAW OF LARGE NUMBERS

BY LANCE GORDON

When I was a cub scout, I engaged in my first encounter with sales. We were selling candy to support the troop and there was a beautiful trophy and prize for the top seller.

I wanted that trophy and the prize. I asked my dad to take the candy to work to see if he could sell it to his employees like many of the other fathers. My dad told me I should do it myself and felt it would be a valuable learning experience. I was disappointed, but I desperately wanted that trophy.

I started knocking on doors after school and began to notice that about one in five contacts resulted in a sale. The rate improved if the weather was bad and the people felt sorry for me having to work in the cold. I went out every night after school and all weekend.

When the winner was announced, I had sold more candy than the rest of the troop combined. This provided a newfound confidence that would later inspire me to successfully sell Christmas cards and Kool-

Aid, build a lawn service customer base, develop snow shoveling jobs and add new customers to my paper route. I knew nothing of the Law of Large Numbers, but I had experienced its power at an early age.

The Law of Large Numbers works without fail, assuming that there is a reasonable number of potential "success units" in the population. By success unit, I mean a person who would be interested in what you are promoting if properly approached and presented with your proposal. Imagine a salesperson trying to sell snowballs in Antarctica. We can assume that there would be no chance of a success unit (selling a snowball) because of the weather and small population.

In probability theory, according to Newey and McFadden[1], the Law of Large Numbers is a theorem that describes the result of performing one experiment a large number of times. The average of the results obtained from a large number of trials will get closer and closer to the true value of the population.

The Law of Large Numbers works best in a large population where there is a large number of "potential" success units. Its impact is widely known in business sectors such as the insurance industry, where there exists both a huge potential market (population) and a need for the service.

Most salespeople are familiar with the phrase, "It's a numbers game." I first heard it when I started my sales career in life and health insurance. I thought I had exhausted all of my contacts. My unit manager believed that repeatedly reminding me that it was a "numbers game" fulfilled his training obligation. But I wasn't sure what he actually meant by this, and it certainly wasn't motivating me to continue working. I figured, roulette is a numbers game. Rolling dice in a game of craps is a numbers game. How could selling insurance have anything to with a game, especially involving numbers?

I launched my insurance career after returning home from four years in the Navy. I had lost touch with most of my friends, and my list of prospects was very small. I kept contacting the same people over and over and had no success. The law of *small* numbers ensured that I would fail. The company was ready to terminate me when I joined the naval reserve. What a change. I suddenly had hundreds of new contacts and many returning veterans who were interested in converting their serviceman's group life insurance. I ended that year by winning the New Agents Performance Award.

My unit manager had actually been giving me some good advice. Unfortunately, he was too involved in meeting his own sales quotas to explain what he actually meant.

Success in any sales and marketing endeavor is not based on luck, as many amateurs believe. It involves the application of mathematical certainty and statistical probability of an event occurring if certain activities are repeated a certain number of times. To be successful in sales or networking, you must understand and believe in the Law of Large Numbers.

It is always on your side, and it varies depending on the potential success units that are present in the population. If only a limited number of people in the population would ever want your product or service, you would have to go through an enormous number of contacts to experience even a modest success rate.

The Law of Large Numbers is not intended to uncover a "needle in the haystack." It assumes enough potential success units in the population to make finding successful experiences a reasonable expectation.

In 1996, I had my first experience with a direct sales networking company that marketed long distance phone service. At my initial training class, the trainer told me that I needed to make a list of everyone I knew. I was told not to edit my list. The list had to contain at least 100 names. From my government audit sampling experience, I could relate to why a list of at least 100 was important, statistically speaking. The trainer explained that every list of 100 would contain one person who would make a car payment for me, one who would make my house payment and one who would make me financially independent. If the Law of Large Numbers were true, then contacting the entire list of 100 should provide at a minimum three good prospects of varying talent.

A strong desire to be successful and a belief in the Law of Large Numbers drove me to contact every person on my list and share my information with them. After ten months, I had contacted all 100 people on the list and even added a few more names. I found five highly successful representatives instead of three and reached six-digit income in my first year. I came to believe even more in the Law of Large numbers and the statistical probability of success when playing the "numbers game."

In 2004, I joined a networking group called BNI. They were in the process of starting a membership drive. Every person in the group was required to make a list of 40 people to invite to a membership campaign called Member Extravaganza.

Their "numbers game" experience was that, for every 40 people you invited, half would accept. Of those twenty who agreed to attend the event, only half – or ten – would attend. Of the half who attended, five would fill out applications to join the group. Of the applications, approximately half would be accepted. That means that out of the original 40 names, only two or three would actually join the chapter.

If those results sound dismal, consider that Business Networking International (BNI) has built the largest networking organization in the world using the Law of Large Numbers. A small success rate has guaranteed them the growth they need. By going through substantial numbers, they have attracted a high caliber membership group and supported their growth. BNI does not attempt to cheat the Law of Large Numbers; rather, they embrace the theory by starting at a high enough number mathematically to guarantee the results they need to grow.

My extensive experience with the power of the Law of Large Numbers helped me build one of the largest tax practices in the north shore suburbs of Milwaukee, Wisconsin. In March of 2009, which was the middle of the tax season, I became involved with a coffee company in Florida called Javalution Coffee Corporation. The company had successfully developed several functional coffees under the name JavaFit that contained a choice of vitamin, weight loss and energy supplements. Combine a unique product with 110 million regular coffee drinkers in the United States, and there exists a high probability that any sample population would contain a large number of success units (interested customers).

I flew down to Fort Lauderdale for a weekend focus group and decided that I wanted to be part of the national expansion plans. One thing was certain: as a CPA, I could not participate in any meaningful way until May. The tax season ended April 15th and I had made plans to spend two weeks in California and Hawaii after the tax season ended to recuperate.

I normally give my clients a "thank you" gift for being loyal and I decided that a package of JavaFit coffee would be a perfect choice. I also brewed JavaFit in the office and offered it to clients when they showed up for their appointments. Without consciously planning a marketing strategy, I had set the Law of Large numbers in motion. In a six week period, I had given away hundreds of free gift packages plus hundreds of cups of brewed coffee.

With my focus on taxes, I was unaware of the impact that the Law of Large Numbers was having on my fledgling coffee business. A strange phenomena began to occur, and I initially failed to understand its' implications. For instance, I began receiving many calls complimenting me on the incredible taste of the Columbian Arabica coffee. People wanted to know where they could buy the product. Some inquired as to whether there were opportunities for them to become involved in the business.

Because of the free gift efforts during the tax season, I spent the last two weeks on vacation in Hawaii returning phone calls to set up coffee orders and train new Independent Coffee Brokers. By the time I returned home, I had become the top income earner in the company and received the JavaFit Affiliate of the Year award at the company convention in Dallas.

The Law of Large Numbers is more pronounced when you have a large population of regular customers who are predisposed to use the product or service. In this case, I was giving coffee to coffee drinkers. They didn't need convincing to drink coffee, just a good reason to try something new and healthy.

My life experiences have convinced me that it doesn't matter what product or service you are trying to market, or how good you do something. What is important is how frequently you do something over a long period of time. In other words, you can do it bad long enough and eventually be successful. I was told many years ago by my father that the road to success and the road to failure were the same road. Success was just farther down the road.

Richard Poe, in his bestselling book, *Wave 3: The New Era in Network Marketing,* predicted the rise of network marketing as a dominating industry of the future because of changes in technology. Technology has improved the level of success that can be experienced in marketing and sales efforts. By going through the necessary exposures required to fulfill the Law of Large Numbers, statistical requirements can be enhanced with technical tools. Websites, webinars, conference calls, automated phone blasts, YouTube videos, DVDs, recorded hotlines, teleguide brochures, social networks, email blasts, and website originated cards are just a few of the innovations that have substantially enhanced the potential for anyone to be successful in today's market.

The power of social networks like Twitter, Facebook and LinkedIn alone have made it much easier to satisfy the large numbers necessary to satisfy the statistical sampling mathematics of the Law of Large Numbers. Instant exposure to massive networks can result in success never before imagined. Combining the high volume exposure with Web-based professional presentations, YouTube videos, information hotlines, and DVD opportunities has reduced the need to have finely-tuned professional sales skills.

While the social networks have had tremendous impact on the ability to interact with large numbers of people, personal contact and building relationships still have an important place in your success. A company called Send Out Cards in Salt Lake City has developed a powerful tool that assists salespeople in prospecting and relationship building. With sophisticated junk mail filters and annoying massive email campaigns, electronic mail has dramatically declined in effectiveness. Send Out Cards has designed a system that starts with selecting a card from their online card catalog and results in a physical card being stamped and sent through the mail. The ability to easily send a large volume of personal cards to prospects, customers and clients provides a powerful tool for building any type of business.

Efficiency can be substantially improved in the Law of Large Numbers by redefining the population. If you knew that ten percent of the population would be interested in what you were promoting, you could start calling names from a phone book and be reasonably confident that one out of ten calls would result in a successful outcome. If you were promoting something that only men could use, then a phone book listing from a men's group would theoretically double your success rate as a redefined population. If your product were geared toward Christian men, then a phone book from a Christian men's group would increase your success rate even more.

A general phone book might have the same names as the Christian men's phone book, but the ratio of success units to fail units is much higher in the latter listing. You could get the same results by making a high volume of calls. Unfortunately, a 90% rejection rate can impact a person's willingness to work through the numbers. Redefining the population mitigates the individual person's varying tolerance for rejection and failure.

Earlier, I noted that many network-marketing companies encourage new members to start with a list of 100 people they know. They are redefining the population to people you are already connected to. The assumption, while not always true, is that your success will be greater if you are contacting people who know and respect you. If your reputation leaves something to be desired, you might be more successful contacting cold market prospects you do not know.

In evaluating my personal abilities, I must admit that I have no special sales skills, product knowledge or other unique talent that would differentiate me from any other networker.

Reflecting back on over thirty years in networking, I can honestly say that I have been successful in every networking endeavor I have attempted. I instinctively knew at an early age that massive action created massive results. There was no magic secret or unique system that would replace methodically working through large enough numbers. I often wonder what course my life would have followed, had my father agreed to take my Cub Scout candy to work and sell it for me.

---

[1] Whitney K. Newey & Daniel McFadden (1994) "Large Sample Estimation and Hypothesis Testing" - *Handbook of Econometrics,* Vol. IV, Chap 36

ABOUT LANCE

Lance Gordon, MS, CPA is the nation's top money earner for JavaFit Healthy Coffee and holds the distinction of being named the first Affiliate of the Year. His meteoric rise to success in network marketing dates back to 1996 with a billion dollar NYSE company called Excel Communications Inc., where he catapulted to the highest promotion level and a six-digit income in his first year. He landed on the Top Performers Council, earned a Top Ten Diamond Award, and became a Circle of Excellence winner over an eight-year career before building immense networks with three more companies.

Lance's sales career started even earlier. At American United Life, the young rep received the New Agents Performance Award his first year with the company. He helped launch a new physician-owned insurance company in Wisconsin and made the President's Club incentive trips his first five years in the business.

A faculty member at the University of Phoenix, Lance teaches accounting and finance courses in the undergraduate and MBA programs. He was an instructor for the Becker CPA Review Course, completed an advanced statistical sampling instructor program with the government, and taught statistics to senior auditors. He was a national training director with Excel Communications and conducted regular direct sales and networking classes at the Milwaukee Training Center and National Conventions in Dallas, Texas. In addition, he served as president of his BNI (Business Networking International) chapter and became a director for the organization.

Lance received his BA in business administration and marketing at Wartburg College, IA, earned a Masters Degree in tax law from the University of Wisconsin-Milwaukee, and a Masters in Information Systems (MIS) degree from North Texas State University.

82

CHAPTER 9

YOUR COMMUNITY, YOUR SUCCESS

BY J.W. DICKS, NICK NANTON AND LINDSAY DICKS

"We have technology, finally, that for the first time in human history allows people to really maintain rich connections with much larger numbers of people."

~ *Pierre Omidyar, founder, eBay*

Steven Spielberg is acknowledged as a legendary filmmaker, as I'm sure you're all aware of. And he's used to getting studios to do what he wants, just because they respect his reputation and his marketing expertise.

As we write this, Spielberg was opening a new movie he's produced – a science-fiction thriller entitled "Super 8." It was scheduled to open on a Friday. But the day before, Thursday morning, it was announced the film would actually open *that very day* in theatres all across America.

...Giving everyone who wants to see that movie a "whole" three or four hours notice.

Now, that opening day can be critical to a movie. Reports of the first-day box office numbers are widely reported through the internet and traditional media, and, if the returns are big, it can make people want to see it more and drive a film to a bigger overall weekend gross. So opening "Super 8" a day early, with that little notice, is already a risky move.

Even riskier... was *how* this crucial announcement was made. Not through a press release, not through new TV spots and totally without any other conventional advertising and marketing...

... but, solely through a Twitter "tweet."

To quote a studio source from the online entertainment site, Deadline.com, the tweet was sent out to "those people who are the more active on social networking sites and most interested in new things and announcing them."

In other words, the *community* that would be most interested in seeing the film – and in spreading the word. They were deemed the most effective in getting out the word – and the best salespeople for the film.

At our Celebrity Branding Agency, we would agree with that decision. We already employ what we call the "3 Pillars of Success" for building a Business Empire. The 3 Pillars are:

1. Positioning

2. Credibility

3. Community

Of these three, we believe that the third is the most important – most certainly, when it comes to building the ultimate network. Community ties everything in your branding together and "spreads the word." Your community already believes in you – so it's like putting your own trained sales force out in the field.

And here's the real secret power of community - when you build one, you build *value*, a lasting value that will give you a consistent and faithful base for years to come.

THE FIRST STEP

You can really base your community on any criteria. After all, a community, at its core, is a group of people with a common thread, whatever that thread might be.

In the past, a community was generally just a group of people who lived near each other. Since they all lived in the same area, they had the same long-term interests and needs. Nowadays, due to the internet's vast influence, most communities have very little to do with geography – they're *online* communities, based on similar interests, hobbies, activities or even based on *hating* the same kind of things (Google "I Hate" and you'll find websites devoted to "I Hate Mountains," "I Hate Cilantro," and even "I Hate Google"!). These communities form by gathering together through social media groups and single-issue websites.

But let's talk about *your* website. Over 99% of the people who visit will never come back. Why? Well, no one really has the complete answer, but we can assume that they get distracted by everything else that's available online and they simply forget about you (especially if your content doesn't change regularly).

Your problem then becomes that, the next time they're looking for a business like yours, they might Google the business category thinking they'll find you. Well, someone else's site might pop up first and, not really having a stake in buying from you, they'll just head over to that web address and hand over their credit card number to the competition. Not good for building *your* business. Especially if your website makes what we consider to be the biggest (and most costly) mistake that most business owners make:

You don't immediately make an effort to capture your first-time visitor's contact info when they arrive at your site.

Now, this is a big mistake that owners of brick-and-mortar businesses make as well – they don't try to capture the information of a prospect that arrives at their physical location. But that doesn't excuse any business websites that don't make this their first priority for a first-time visitor – because, again, the whole idea is to make sure that a first-time visitor isn't also a *last*-time visitor.

You might say to yourself, those people probably weren't really in the market for what I have to sell - otherwise, they would come back to the site on their own. Well, again, they might not come back to *your* site to make that purchase – so that's good logic only if you care about the here and now. And it's great logic, if you don't want to be in business in a year or two.

Here's why we say that. There's an experiment that we try when speaking to large crowds. We'll ask, "How many of you are looking to buy a car this month?" You'll get maybe one or two people raising a hand, depending on the size of the room. Next we ask, "How many of you are going to buy a car in the next six months to a year?" Now, about twenty percent of the people raise their hands. Finally, we ask, "How many people in this room are going to buy a car in the next three to five years?"

And everyone's hands go up.

The point is, if our business was selling cars and we just walked away from this giant group because only one or two of them want to buy a vehicle *now*, we'd be shooting ourselves in our metaphorical foot. *That's because at some point, all of them will be potential customers.* Not everyone is ready to buy this second. In fact, as our experiment repeatedly demonstrates, the majority of people *aren't* ready.

Your business is presumably about the long run, however. And gathering that contact info at your website is important to that long run.

That's because it gives you the ability to control the conversation.

With that contact info, you put them into your community. And, once they're in your community, you can continue to "talk" to them and educate them after they've left your site. You have the ability to demonstrate to them on an ongoing basis your expertise and authority in your area of business. And subtly, over time, you become the go-to guy when they need what you have to sell, because you're the most trusted resource that they're acquainted with.

When you're building your own virtual community, the common thread is *you*. You're at the center of it, you control what gets said, you create the image you want created and they're the passive receivers of that image. What's interesting is that after a while, if for some reason you get attacked online, you'll find to your delight and surprise that this community will actually rise up and defend you.

But none of that good stuff happens unless you get that all-important email address and put that person on your list. The fact that they came to your website at all demonstrates an interest in your business – otherwise they'd be on Facebook playing Farmville. And just because they're not ready to buy now doesn't mean they won't buy later – in fact, the opposite is true. If they visit you in the first place, there's a reason.

… Which means there's also an opportunity.

By capturing their email address, you're able to deal head-on with their indecisiveness about buying. You now have the opportunity to build an irrefutable case that you are the best choice to deliver what they want – which means, when they're finally ready to whip out their credit card, you're in prime position to get their business.

As time goes on and your contact list lengthens, you'll find that you have an entire community of prospects engaged in this conversation that you control – which means you've laid the all-important ground-work for future sales of your products and/or services.

CONTINUING TO BUILD YOUR COMMUNITY

While there's no better way to begin your community than by capturing the contact info of visitors to your site, there are other effective methods of gathering more people in your circle as well. Keep in mind what we said at the beginning of this chapter – a common thread holds together a community. That thread is the key to building yours.

For example, if you run a business that manufactures and sells high-end video equipment and lighting, you'll want to build a community of professionals in the TV and film production industry. Furthermore, you want to educate them on why you manufacture your products the way you do and how your quality products can help them achieve optimal performance.

You should attempt to build such communities both online, through social media and blogging, and in the "real world." Here are a few suggestions on how to do just that:

1. CREATE A COMMUNITY BASED ON YOUR POTENTIAL CUSTOMERS' AREAS OF INTERESTS.

As many business experts tell you to do, you should create a profile of your "perfect customer." That profile will give you all-important clues as to what kinds of people would be receptive to the products and services you provide – as well as what their other interests might be. This gives you the foundation to explore, online and offline, groups of people that might fit into your community, which will probably be formed around a specific niche tailored to your business.

Online, these groups often center on forums which allow for discussions of various topics that could be relevant to your business. A quick Google search should turn up the kind of groups you're looking for. Offline, these types of groups may show up in the form of hobby enthusiasts, specific business associations or other trade organizations.

These groups may not be directly related to what your business is all about – but there may be enough of a crossover-appeal to get them interested in your specific niche. For example, if you're selling video game guides and books, you might want to check out World of Warcraft groups or other game-specific gatherings both in your area and online.

2. IF THERE'S ALREADY A COMMUNITY FOR YOUR AREA OF INTEREST, CREATE A NEW ONE WITH A UNIQUE SPIN.

There may already be a thriving community that fulfills the needs of your specific niche. Maybe those video game guides you're selling are already written for World of Warcraft groups, of which there are about a billion.

That means you should drill deeper to create a sub-niche that still has some impact for your primary market. For example, focusing on World of Warcraft *secrets* would probably entice some members of the community to also be involved in your community. If your niche is cooking, finding a sub-niche of a style of cooking that's just catching on could be effective. Whatever it is, your new community should seem innovative and cutting-edge as well as offer something a little different, so that it doesn't seem like a dated copy of some other group.

3. THE MORE EXPOSURE, THE BETTER.

Remember that creating your own community is basically the wind-up to a pitch in a baseball game – you still have to actually throw the ball!

That means you can't just build your group and take it easy. The reason you built it in the first place is to educate your community in your niche and establish yourself as the expert – that's how you convert the prospects in your community to customers.

Again, you shouldn't be trying to sell to these people directly – they get enough of that in their everyday lives. They have no reason to stick around and listen to your sales pitch if they don't have to. Instead, you should be creating value for them in the form of information in the areas they're interested in. As you create that value, their trust in you and their willingness to eventually hire you or buy from you will only grow exponentially.

That requires you to put yourself out there – with blogs, videos, or even simple quick tips on a Twitter feed. The more you engage and participate, the better it is for you and your business. After all, it's your community – you're the leader, so it's up to you to lead.

A final note – hopefully, your business reflects your personal interests. When you have a passion for what you do, your community will see it as genuine and respond favorably to that passion, because they presumably share it.

That means you'll create many authentic relationships and form genuine bonds with your community. Nothing beats the synergy that comes out of business and personal objectives lining up. And nothing beats having a community where you can relax, be yourself and not have to think about making sales.

That's the way you build true value!

ABOUT NICK

An Emmy Award Winning Director and Producer, Nick Nanton, Esq., is known as The Celebrity Lawyer and Agent to top Celebrity Experts for his role in developing and marketing business and professional experts, through personal branding, media, marketing and PR to help them gain credibility and recognition for their accomplishments. Nick is recognized as the nation's leading expert on personal branding as Fast Company Magazine's Expert Blogger on the subject and lectures regularly on the topic at the University of Central Florida. His book *Celebrity Branding You®* has been selected as the textbook on personal branding at the University.

The CEO of The Dicks + Nanton Celebrity Branding Agency, Nick is an award winning director, producer and songwriter who has worked on everything from large scale events to television shows with the likes of Bill Cosby, President George H.W. Bush, **Brian Tracy**, Michael Gerber and many more.

Nick is recognized as one of the top thought-leaders in the business world and has co-authored 10 best-selling books, including the breakthrough hit *Celebrity Branding You!®*.

Nick serves as publisher of Celebrity Press™, a publishing company that produces and releases books by top Business Experts. CelebrityPress has published books by Brian Tracy, **Mari Smith**, Ron Legrand and many other celebrity experts and Nick has led the marketing and PR campaigns that have driven more than 300 authors to Best-Seller status. Nick has been seen in USA Today, The Wall St. Journal, Newsweek, Inc. Magazine, The New York Times, Entrepreneur® Magazine, **FastCompany.com** and has appeared on ABC, NBC, CBS, and FOX television affiliates around the country speaking on subjects ranging from branding, marketing and law, to American Idol.

Nick is a member of the Florida Bar, holds a JD from the University of Florida Levin College of Law, as well as a BSBA in Finance from the University of Florida's Warrington College of Business. Nick is a voting member of The National Academy of Recording Arts & Sciences (NARAS, Home to The GRAMMYs), a member of The National Academy of Television Arts & Sciences (Home to the Emmy Awards) co-founder of the National Academy of Best-Selling Authors, a 6-time Telly Award winner, and spends his spare time working with Young Life, Downtown Credo Orlando, Florida Hospital and rooting for the Florida Gators with his wife Kristina and their three children, Brock, Bowen and Addison.

ABOUT LINDSAY

Lindsay Dicks helps her clients tell their stories in the online world. Being brought up around a family of marketers, but a product of Generation Y, Lindsay naturally gravitated to the new world of on-line marketing. Lindsay began freelance writing in 2000 and soon after launched her own PR firm that thrived by offering an in-your-face "Guaranteed PR" that was one of the first of its type in the nation.

Lindsay's new media career is centered on her philosophy that "people buy people." Her goal is to help her clients build a relationship with their prospects and customers. Once that relationship is built and they learn to trust them as the expert in their field then they will do business with them. Lindsay also built a patent-pending process called "circular marketing" that utilizes social media marketing, content marketing and search engine optimization to create online "buzz" for her clients that helps them to convey their business and personal story. Lindsay's clientele span the entire business map and range from doctors and small business owners to Inc 500 CEOs.

Lindsay is a graduate of the University of Florida. She is the CEO of CelebritySites™, an online marketing company specializing in social media and online personal brand-ing. Lindsay is also a multi-best-selling author including the best-selling book "Power Principles for Success" which she co-authored with Brian Tracy. She was also se-lected as one of America's PremierExperts™ and has been quoted in Newsweek, the Wall Street Journal, USA Today, Inc Magazine as well as featured on NBC, ABC, and CBS television affiliates speaking on social media, search engine optimization and making more money online. Lindsay was also recently brought on FOX 35 News as their Online Marketing Expert.

Lindsay, a national speaker, has shared the stage with some of the top speakers in the world such as Brian Tracy, Lee Milteer, Ron LeGrand, Arielle Ford, David Bullock, Brian Horn, Peter Shankman and many others. Lindsay was also a Producer on the Emmy nominated film Jacob's Turn.

You can connect with Lindsay at:

Lindsay@CelebritySites.com
www.twitter.com/LindsayMDicks
www.facebook.com/LindsayDicks

ABOUT JW

JW Dicks, Esq. is an attorney, best-selling author, entrepreneur and business advisor to top Celebrity Experts. He has spent his entire 35-year career building successful businesses for himself and clients by creating business development and marketing campaigns that have produced sales of over a billion dollars in products and services. His professional versatility gives him a unique insight into his clients' businesses to see untapped opportunities to capitalize on, allowing him to use his knowledge of how to structure and position their business to take advantage of them.

He is the Senior Partner of Dicks & Nanton P.A., a unique membership-based, legal and business consulting firm representing clients who want to expand their business. JW helps his clients position their business and personal brand to take advantage of new vertical income streams they haven't tapped into, and shows them how to use associations, franchises, area-exclusive licensing, coaching programs, info-marketing, joint ventures, and multi-channel marketing to take advantage of them.

In addition to consulting and mentoring clients, JW is also a successful entrepreneur and America's leading expert on personal branding for business development. He is co-founder of the Celebrity Branding Agency, representing clients who want to get major media coverage, marketing and PR, and position themselves as the leading expert in their field. His Best-Selling book, *Celebrity Branding You!*, is in its third edition and new editions are currently being published for specific industries. He also writes a monthly column for Fast Company Magazine's Expert Blogg on personal branding, and has written hundreds of articles, blogs and special reports on the subject.

JW has led national conferences and conventions and has spoken to over 160,000 business leaders on branding, business joint ventures, capital formation, investing, and legal and business growth strategies. He is the Best Selling author of 22 business and legal books – including *How to Start a Corporation and Operate in Any State* (a 50 Volume set), *Celebrity Branding You!*, *Power Principles for Success*, *Moonlight Investing*, *The Florida Investor*, *Mutual Fund Investing Strategies*, *The Small Business Legal Kit*, *The 100 Best Investments For Your Retirement*, *Financial CPR*, *Operation Financial Freedom*, *Game Changers*, *How to Buy and Sell Real Estate*, *Ignite Your Business Transform Your World*, and more.

JW is the editor and publisher of The Celebrity Experts® Insider, delivered to clients in over 15 countries, and serves as the guide for entrepreneurs and professionals who are leading experts in their field. He has been called the "Expert to the Experts" and has appeared in USA Today, The Wall Street Journal, Newsweek, Inc. Magazine, The New York Times, Entrepreneur Magazine, and on ABC, NBC, CBS, and FOX television affiliates. Recently, JW was honored with an Emmy nomination as Executive Producer for the film, *Jacob's Turn*.

JW's business address is Orlando, FL and his play address is at his beach house where he spends as much time as he can with Linda, his wife of 39 years, their family, and two Yorkies. His major hobby is fishing, although the fish are rumored to be safe.

CHAPTER 10

TO BOW OR TO SHAKE HANDS?
– CULTURAL DIFFERENCES AND NETWORKING ETIQUETTE

BY DR. IVAN MISNER

We now live in a fully global society where it is imperative to have an awareness of cultural differences as they relate to networking etiquette. We often notice differences within our own states. Certainly between regions of the nation; but what about businesses that are networking with businesses in other parts of the world? We actually cross cultures with every person we meet.

In business, when we concentrate on similarities with each other, the differences aren't that important. Problems arise when the differences appear to be all there are. When entrepreneurs focus on the perceived differences between each other in business, these differences can become stumbling blocks to developing a strong relationship, which is, after all, the ultimate goal of networking. When you factor in differences in communication and behavioral styles it exacerbates the perceived differences.

It becomes very easy for a "them" vs. "us" situation to develop. People then focus on the problems as evidence that the differences do actually exist and make it more difficult to work together. This dynamic can greatly multiply the cultural differences that naturally do occur, whether you are talking about an East coast firm doing business with a West coast supplier or a Western business negotiating with an Eastern firm.

It is important to find things that bring us together, ...things that are similar for us all. For example, we all speak the language of referrals and we all want to do business based on trust. This transcends many cultural differences.

I have mentioned before that some resist structured referral marketing programs, claiming that it's "too American" to which I have replied, "The law of reciprocity" is about the least 'American' concept around! We aren't teaching our business graduates to focus on what they can give as they support each other in developing businesses. On the contrary, they are more or less being taught to win as much as you can… dog eat dog…you get the idea." I submit that as we move into a more global arena of networking, the similarities between us will become more and more evident as we teach business owners to speak the language of referrals.

That said – we should be aware of and prepared for, some of these particular cultural differences that can affect the way we network with other cultures. They are sometimes as simple as the way we hand out a business card, to as complex as the study of proxemics and the usage of specific idioms.

Networking in today's market takes finesse and knowledge of the culture in which you are networking. I am currently working on a new book with co-author Sam Schwartz on the subject of networking etiquette. There are a lot of entrepreneurs who study networking, but I want to take a look at cultural nuances we need to be aware of.

Here are three areas where cultural differences mandate a closer look at networking etiquette:

1. BUSINESS CARD ETIQUETTE

Exchanging business cards is an essential part of most cultures. In most Asian countries, after a person has introduced him or herself and bowed, the business card ceremony begins. In Japan, this is called *mei-shi*. The card is presented to the other person with the front side facing upwards toward the recipient. Offering the card with both hands holding the top corners of the card demonstrates respect to the other person.

The business card etiquette is much more ceremonious in the Asian culture than it is to us here in America. It is truly an extension of the individual and is treated with respect. Things like tucking it into a pocket after receiving it, writing on it, bending or folding it in any way, or even looking at it again after you have first accepted it and looked at it, are not considered polite and can insult your fellow Asian networker.

2. CONSIDERATION OF "PERSONAL SPACE"

When networking and meeting others with whom you wish to pursue a word-of-mouth marketing paradigm, it's very important to respect the cultural boundaries relating to personal space.

The science of proxemics (the study of our use of space) really is fascinating. For example, a Yale dissertation written by William Ickinger in the 1980's revealed that female pairs stand closer to one another than female/male pairs, who stand closer to one another than male/male pairs. Although this separation was small (a difference of less than 3 inches), the predicted pattern listed above was observed consistently during the study.

It's crucial to understand the subtle, unspoken dynamics of personal space. Someone might not even be able to put a finger on what it is that sours the business relationship, when in reality, it's nothing more than discomfort from having his or her own "bubble" encroached upon. Some cultural dynamics are fine with close personal interaction, while others demand a bigger bubble. This is not a point to underestimate.

There are three basic separations to consider when taking proxemics into account. For Americans, they typically are: public space (ranges from 12 to 25 feet), social space (ranges from 4 to 10 feet), personal space (ranges from 2 to 4 feet), and intimate space (ranges out to one foot).

In Saudi Arabia, their social space equates to our intimate space and you might find yourself recoiling while your business associate may get the impression that you are stand-offish. In the Netherlands, this might be reversed due to the fact that their personal space equates to our social space. Do your homework and be sensitive to cultural differences in this area. You may find it interesting to take a look at even when dealing with business people here in the USA, as we mix more and more with professionals from other cultures in our everyday dealings.

3. USE OF SLANG

When using slang in a business environment, you might want to keep in mind that what means one thing to us might have no meaning, or a very different meaning, to a business man or woman from another culture. I have some personal experiences in this area, some humorous, others quite embarrassing!

One of my business associates and I were talking with his business partner from South Africa. Even though we were all speaking English, one of the phrases we used caused his partner to go completely silent. We had both reassured him that we would keep him in the loop regarding some aspect of the business. It wasn't until two weeks later that he re-established contact with us and shared that he finally understood what we really had meant. You see, in his dialect, we had told him that we would keep him pregnant! Not at all what we had intended, I can assure you.

In another case, we learned that some European countries don't have a direct translation for "word of mouth", so they translate it to "mouth to mouth". I had to explain that this has a totally different connotation in the USA. There were a lot of people over here getting quite excited about this "mouth-to-mouth" marketing taking place in Europe!

It also took me a few minutes to figure out what my Australian associates were saying when upon meeting me, they all said (incredibly fast): "G'daymight". I finally had to ask and was told: "Oh, for our American friend here – we are saying 'good day mate'."

If you have the ability to consult with someone in that country who is familiar with that culture before interacting with the business people, jump at it. It was invaluable to me to be able to have my Israeli Director in BNI, Sam Schwartz, coach me regarding the Orthodox Jewish custom of not shaking hands with someone of the opposite gender. He and his associates effectively coached me on how to recognize when a business woman was an Orthodox Jew, by noting if she was wearing any type of head covering (a normal hat would not have been recognized by me as this type of indicator, had he not coached me in this), or a knee-length skirt with opaque tights worn underneath so that no skin was visible. Again, I would not have even noticed that this was any type of indication, but he was able to clue me in.

As you have the opportunity to network with others from different cultures and countries, don't hesitate because you are not sure how your actions will be interpreted. Do your homework ahead of time. One great resource for information on customs and business etiquette is: www.ExecutivePlanet.com. When I have the opportunity to travel to another country to do business, I often check in here to be sure I'm not going to make an inappropriate gesture, remark or some other offensive behavior.

Networking basics are universal; with some care for taking into account those cultural nuances that will give you a 'leg up', you can be assured that your networking etiquette will be appreciated here at home and as your business takes you into other countries.

ABOUT IVAN

Dr. Ivan Misner is the Founder & Chairman of BNI (*www.bni.com*), the world's largest business networking organization. BNI was founded in 1985. The organization now has over 6,000 chapters throughout every populated continent of the world. Last year alone, BNI generated 6.5 million referrals resulting in $2.8 billion dollars worth of business for its members.

Dr. Misner's Ph.D. is from the University of Southern California. He is a *New York Times* Bestselling author who has written over 12 books, including his latest one, called *Networking Like a Pro*, which can be viewed at: *www.IvanMisner.com*. He is a monthly columnist for Entrepreneur.com and is the Senior Partner for the Referral Institute – an international referral training company *(www.referralinstitute.com)*, with trainers around the world. In addition, he has taught business management and social capital courses at several universities throughout the United States.

Called the "Father of Modern Networking" by CNN and the *"Networking Guru"* by Entrepreneur magazine, Dr. Misner is considered to be one of the world's leading experts on business networking, and has been a keynote speaker for major corporations and associations throughout the world. He has been featured in *The L.A. Times, The Wall Street Journal,* and *The New York Times,* as well as numerous TV and radio shows, including *CNN, CNBC,* and the *BBC* in London.

Dr. Misner is on the Board of Trustees for the University of LaVerne, CA. He is also the Founder of the BNI-Misner Charitable Foundation and was recently named *"Humanitarian of the Year"* by a Southern California newspaper.

He is married and lives with his wife Elisabeth and their three children in Claremont, CA. *In his spare time(!!!),* he is also an amateur magician and has a black belt in karate.

CHAPTER 11

SIX NETWORKING "SECRETS" FROM A CANDLE LADY

BY WENDY LLOYD CURLEY

H i. I'm Wendy and I work in network marketing. Have I lost you already?

Of course I have. The words "network marketing" are fluffy and with an introduction like that, you don't know anything about me or what I sell.

Hi. I'm Wendy the Candle Lady and I sell beautiful, fragranced candles.

That's better. Direct, clear, and honest. Now you know what I do.

When I was asked to write a chapter for this book, I instantly knew what I wanted to share with you. I realised that I have cracked a problem in networking that many people struggle with everyday. So in this chapter, I'm going to share all I know and let you know my "secrets" to networking success.

The "secrets" are to be passionate, focus on the primary product or service you offer, prioritize quality over quantity, form relationships, develop trust, and persist.

This chapter includes information and insight that will help everyone succeed at networking, but if you are in network marketing (also known as direct selling, multi-level marketing, or party plan), you should pay particular attention. No matter what product or service you sell (candles, kitchen ware, cosmetics, cleaning supplies, steak knives, insurance plans, vitamins, clothes, books, software, sex toys, or telecommunications services, to name a few), my "secrets" will give you the confidence to meet and network with *anyone*, from *any* background, and in *any* profession... without either of you feeling uncomfortable.

Really.

SECRET 1:
BE PASSIONATE ABOUT YOUR PRODUCT OR SERVICE

Do you have to use the product or service you are selling? No. Not if you don't need it.

But you do have to be passionate about it.

No matter what you sell, you need to understand it from top to bottom and be able to communicate to others the reasons why your product or service will make their lives better. Share information about how to use your product or service to get the most value out of it. Understand your competitors, substitutes and alternatives. Give examples and testimonials from current clients.

Sell the sizzle.

Me? I sell candles. I use candles. I love candles. I love the fragrance and the ambiance. I have a fantastic smelling home with beautiful candles and diffusers all around me. And I love to talk about candles to others. I buy candles from other candle companies. I compare candles. I know how to get every penny's worth of value out of a candle and I enjoy teaching others how to do the same.

I am that passionate.

It makes me a better business owner.

Focusing on the products I sell and being passionate about them also makes me a better networker.

Are you passionate about your product or service? You better be.

SECRET 2:
FOCUS ON ONE MESSAGE:
THE PRODUCT OR SERVICE YOU SELL

As business people, we all have a variety of messages we want to get across. Certainly a 30-60 second commercial is not enough time to tell people at a business networking event everything you want to say.

But it is enough time.

You have to have focus.

You need one message. Multiple messages will not be heard. Only one will break through.

Make it about the product or service you sell. Use the opportunity to promote your product or service. Don't clutter the message. Keep it simple.

The problem is that we want to get the biggest bang for our networking buck. So we try to fit everything in. In the end, it just comes out sounding rehearsed (or memorized), insincere, probably rushed, and selfish.

So, my "secret" is: lead with your products and services, then share more about your products and services, and then sum up about your products and services.

They will remember you.

NETWORK MARKETERS, LISTEN UP

Secret 2 was the *Eureka!* moment for me. Once I focused on my candles, I found everything else started to work. I got more referrals. I talked to more people. I got more orders. In the end, I'll meet more people who will be right to approach for a discussion about the business opportunity.

Here are two additional tips for network marketers:

1. Do not ever hide the fact that you are in a network marketing company; that is dishonest. You can mention the company. You can even say that you are a distributor, agent, consultant, or licensee. All I am saying is that *you should not say that you are looking for other people* to start their own network marketing businesses. In a business networking situation that is simply a major turn-off. Do that in a more targeted and personal way *once you have identified a reason* to make the offer.

   Market your product or service with passion; your business will be strong and then the business opportunity will be even more attractive.

2. "Oh. I get it. It's a Pyramid..."

   Actually, there is a big difference between a pyramid scheme and network marketing.

   Is it just semantics?

   Not really. A pyramid scheme is the name for an illegal, non-sustainable business model that involves the exchange of money primarily for *enrolling other people into the scheme,* often without any tangible product or service being delivered. On the other hand, network marketing is a legal, sustainable business model that creates value through tangible product and service sales.

   If the word pyramid is used, I always educate people about the difference. I don't get defensive about it; I simply share the differences. I have found the information to be well received.

SECRET 3:
QUALITY IS MORE IMPORTANT THAN QUANTITY

A few years ago, I attended a conference specifically designed for micro-business owners. Each of us had come to the event excited to meet other people who worked in small or solo businesses. We were there to learn about many things that had the potential to make our businesses stronger. One of the sessions I attended was a discussion about networking. The discussion that day helped me formulate my entire outlook on the power, potential, and possibilities of good networking.

To be an effective networker, it's not the quantity of people you meet; it's the quality of the relationships you develop. And it takes time.

Until that day, I had attended business networking events and almost always left disappointed.

Why?

Because I had paid to be there, had invested an hour, had worked the room, had talked to a dozen people, had given out 20 or more business cards, and had left with no leads.

What a waste.

So after I attended the seminar, I tried a different approach.

I still paid to be there, and I still invested an hour of my time. But I didn't work the room. I didn't even work the table. Even smaller: I worked the lady to my right. We talked for the whole hour. I learned a lot about her and she learned a lot about me. We exchanged cards and the next week we caught up for a coffee. I asked about her business and she asked about mine. She invited me to another networking group that she thought would appreciate my candles. She also introduced me to an architect she knew. Over the last year, I've gotten hundreds of leads and thousands of dollars in sales from the people I've met through her. I've referred people to her, too.

One contact.

One friend.

In fact... that is how I approach networking now... meeting new friends.

See it's the quality of the contact that counts, not the quantity.

SECRET 4:
ASK QUESTIONS AND LISTEN TO DEVELOP RELATIONSHIPS

So you don't want to start the conversation by talking all about you. What do you do?

You ask them about them.

It's really simple. It's not small talk. It's genuine. You introduce yourself and then ask them questions like what do they do, how are they involved, what brought them to the event, how many kids do they have, how long have they owned their business, have they been to the event before?

Ask anything you really want to know.

And then *listen* to the answers.

It's the listening part where you might get tripped up. You see, you might be thinking about yourself again. How can you make them talk about you, ask about you. How can you get a word in? Who else is in the room that you need to meet?

But that's not what you should be thinking. You've asked a question. Listen to the answer.

Then follow-up. Ask another question.

Hold back from talking about yourself... unless of course, they have asked you a question in return.

The key is to really, truly care what they say and to really truly understand where they are coming from. Get to know them and then you will be able to move on to secret 5.

SECRET 5:
GIVE TO DEVELOP TRUST

The real key to networking is to go to every network event without expectations of getting anything in return. My strategy is that I go to each event to see how I can help others get what they want.

In effect, I'm offering my own personal and business network to whoever I meet.

"We're about to renovate our apartment."

Me: Have you got plans drawn up already? (Refer designers, architects, builders.)

"My child wants to learn piano."

Me: Have you got a teacher in mind? (Refer to music stores or people.)

"We're about to add a few people in our call centre."

Me: Have you started the recruiting process yet? (Refer to recruiters or candidates.)

"I've had a sore shoulder since playing tennis last week."

Me: What treatments have you tried? (Refer to doctors, massage therapists.)

"My company provides financial planning services to people who have just been laid off.

Me: May I have your card? I have a friend who thinks that might happen to her soon.

Did you notice that I always offered something? Something appropriate. Something targeted. A person who could help. A person I've done business with. A possible client.

Give, give, give.

Trust is developed when you come across as genuinely interested in their needs. When you offer support. When you get them results.

And it is even more powerful when you have asked for nothing in return.

SECRET 6:
PERSIST

You cannot expect to develop relationships or trust in one event.

If the group meets regularly, and if you enjoy the group, you should prioritise attending the events regularly. Developing relationships happens over time. Seeing people regularly will automatically help you develop trust. Attend once and the group will not remember you at the next meeting. Attend four meetings in a row and if you cannot make the fifth meeting, people will probably wonder where you are.

And they will care.

In any case, but especially if the event is a one-off event, you need to follow-up with the people you have connected with. Send an email with the names and numbers of the people you referred. Send a note in the mail thanking them for their time. Call them the next week and ask them to another event that they would benefit from.

Don't be fake. Be genuine. Follow-up for a reason.

But you must follow-up.

Persist.

HOW NETWORK MARKETERS FAIL IN NETWORKING

Network marketers get a bad reputation because many participants approach new contacts with their sales pitch to "join" the business rather than developing a relationship with the new person and making a reasonable, trustworthy, and tailored presentation.

Why do network marketers do this?

I contend it is because of two statements I hear often in training designed for network marketers:

(a) Offer the opportunity to everyone and

(b) It is a numbers game.

I am going to politely disagree with those statements.

Don't offer the opportunity to everyone.

Not everyone is right for the business. I contend that it is not appropriate to walk up to a complete stranger at a business networking event and offer them another, unrelated business opportunity. Without any relationship, any trust, or any background, that approach is sure to backfire more than it will succeed.

It is not a numbers game.

It is a business, and, to build an effective team of network marketers, it is not about numbers, it is about interest, need, and fit. You can only discover those qualifications by developing a relationship. Qualifying individuals for interest, need, and fit is a perfectly acceptable practice.

The number of people buying your products is the best testament to how good your business opportunity is. Put your attention on the product sales, listen to your clients, and offer the opportunity to the right people at the right time.

Put simply, market your product with passion and your business becomes more attractive.

But she said....

I can already see the comments rolling in about how wrong I am. So please allow me to clarify.

I am not saying that network marketers should avoid discussing the opportunity for someone to start a network marketing business in *every* situation. I am saying that network marketers should refrain from discussing the business opportunity when they are introducing themselves in a business networking environment.

I'm not saying that it is inappropriate for a network marketer to mention the business opportunity when he or she is presenting to a targeted audience.

I'm not saying it is inappropriate to let people know about the business opportunity when conducting a professional demonstration. When I do a home demonstration about the candles I sell, I certainly let it be known that I am one of many distributors for the candles and that if anyone in the room is interested in learning about how to become a distributor themselves, I would be happy to provide them with information.

AND THEY ALL NETWORKED HAPPILY EVER AFTER....

What I have shared with you are the "secrets" of my success at networking. Every day I work on them, hone them, and try new things. But the principles I've shared with you here are constant.

1. Be passionate about your product or service.
2. Focus on one message in a new networking situation.
3. Quality is more important than quantity.
4. Ask questions and listen to develop relationships.
5. Give to develop trust.
6. Persist.

For network marketers, remember, market your product with passion; your business will be strong, and then the business opportunity will be even more attractive.

ABOUT WENDY

Wendy Lloyd Curley is passionate about candles. She runs her own business in Australia, selling PartyLite candles, fragrances, and homewares as an independent consultant since 2005 and as a leader since 2007. She consistently leads her region in personal and unit sales and sponsoring, has earned four consecutive incentive trips overseas for herself and her husband, and has achieved numerous sales excellence awards.

Wendy credits four things for her success as a business owner: her passion for her product, her willingness to try new things, her continuous quest to learn, and her flair for networking.

Wendy grew up in Scottsdale, Arizona. She worked in the hospitality industry in both the US and Australia until she went back to university to earn three degrees: Bachelor of Science (Arizona State University), MBA (Arizona State University), and Master of International Management (The American Graduate School of International Management). She then worked in telecommunications for 10 years before her entrepreneurial spirit took over. She founded WLC Enterprises in 2005.

Wendy now lives with her family in Sydney, Australia and works as a writer, speaker, musician, and candle lady. She can be contacted via her website at: www.wendythecandlelady.com.

CHAPTER 12

BUILD IT, EDUCATE IT, MOTIVATE IT & ACTIVATE IT!

BY PAULA FRAZIER

I am a 4th generation entrepreneur. Until I was 26, our family was blessed to have 5 generations walking this Earth that knew, loved and learned from one another. Amazingly enough, they were all husbands and wives working side-by-side – building their businesses to support their families.

Looking back, I realize how valuable it was for me to experience the ups and downs that every business goes through and the lessons that follow. My great-grandparents taught me that sometimes you have to roll up your sleeves and get dirty to get the job done. My grandparents helped me understand that you have to work incredibly hard to earn your place... especially in a successful family business. My parents educated me in the fine art of negotiation. They used to take me to the

113

flea market and show me how to spend $5 bucks like it was $50 dollars.

It's interesting to know that nearly every generation had children that worked in the family business; but there was always one that struck out on their own. I was that one.

A little over ten years ago, I found my place in the referral marketing industry as a trainer, coach and consultant. I help people build their business by developing powerful personal networks that produce high quality referrals.

Recent statistics show that 78% of small business owners are counting on over 90% of their business to come by referral… and they don't have a plan to make it happen. The problem is that most entrepreneurs consider themselves to be "natural networkers." You can be a natural networker, but there is a science to purposefully producing qualified referrals.

Your net-WORTH is directly related to the strength of your net-WORK when you are building your business by referral!

Successfully establishing the *ultimate* network requires that you strategically and relationally build it, educate it, motivate it, and then activate it!

BUILD IT!

Whether you walk into a boardroom or a ballroom, you are in a position to build your network.

First, you've got to make sure that your behavior supports your intentions. We attend networking events with every intention to net-WORK. Instead we net-sit, net-eat, net-drink, net-talk and as a result we net-nothing for our business which leads us to the unreasonable conclusion that networking is a waste of time.

Take a good hard look around the room the next time you go to a Chamber event. Some people are running around with their tail-feathers on fire, hugging and kissing a lot of unsuspecting victims. A number of people are standing guard around the perimeter of the room like good little soldiers content to listen and take it all in. Others are satisfied spending most of their time with people they already know. And then there are the self-proclaimed important people; the ones that stand there with their arms crossed waiting for people to come to them.

From the outside it looks like sheer madness, but potentially it's a room full of referrals so you've got to get in there. The key is to recognize where you fit in and then effectively engage the others. Tony Alessandra's Platinum Rule has served me well in these situations - *Treat others they way they prefer to be treated.* When you begin interacting and communicating with people in a way that is most comfortable for them, great things will happen for you and your business.

When you're building a network you must also resist the temptation to qualify and disqualify each person you meet. Just because they aren't a prospective client for you doesn't mean that they aren't a valuable resource for someone you know. We're not just building a network for ourselves; it must also serve the people that make up our network.

I hosted a workshop a couple of years ago. Everyone in attendance pretty much looked the same; high end suits, hair done, shiny shoes, fancy phones with laptops in tow…except one guy. He was wearing uniform pants, a sweatshirt, work boots and a ponytail. Almost no one spoke to him. They disregarded Jeremy because he was different.

The one person that did take the time to connect with him struck gold. He learned that Jeremy was an auto mechanic. Not just any auto mechanic; Jeremy was one of two Master Certified Porsche Mechanic's in all of Southwestern Virginia. Do you think that some of his clients may resemble our target market?

Unless and until we have all the business we need, none of us have the luxury of excluding or ostracizing people. After all, *variety is the spice of life…* it's also one of the keys to building a diverse network. Next time you attend an event, find a person in the room that no one else is talking to and start digging. You might strike gold!

Finally, you must attend events with purpose… the purpose of connecting with people to build and maintain an active network. How many people do you want to meet? Which industries do they represent? What purpose will they serve as a member of your network?

The most successful networkers I know go with goals and employ relational strategies. Try this 'easy as 1-2-3' approach at the next event you attend:

1. Identify a person in the room that no one else is talking to and engage them.
2. Find out who they are, what they do and offer a little bit about yourself.
3. Agree to follow up (as appropriate) and share your goal:
   a. "I've enjoyed meeting you."
   b. "I'd really like to learn more about you and your business. I'll give you a call in the next few days so we can schedule a time that works for your schedule" OR "I've really enjoyed learning more about you and your business."
   c. "My goal is to meet 4-5 new people at events like this. Is there someone here that you know that you'd be willing to introduce me to?"

Before you know it, you will be getting 'danced around the room' one strategic introduction at a time.

EDUCATE IT!

Once you begin to establish a network of people that know who you are and what you do, it's time to teach them how to refer you. You must empower them with your clear, repeatable, memorable word-of-mouth message so they can consistently share it every time they have an opportunity to promote you.

A great place to start is with an "I help" statement. It's a quick, effective way for one of your referral partners to share the benefits of your products and services without sounding too formal or transactional.

For example, not a day goes by that I don't hear someone complaining about his or her computer. I don't have to be technologically savvy to offer them a solution. All I have to do is share a "help" statement from the appropriate person in my network:

> *"I know how frustrating it can be when your computer gets temperamental. I'd be glad to introduce you to my good friend, Celie, with Fast-teks. She **helps** people and their technology work better together."*

It's intended to peak their interest and encourage them to want to learn more. At this point in the conversation, people typically drop their guard and become open to the possibilities. No hard sales tactics. You are simply recommending someone that you know and trust to satisfy their potential need.

Another great educational tool is your Unique Selling Position (USP). We tend to sound like one of those late night infomercials when we attempt to promote others. They slice! They dice! They julienne and fry! And if you act now you can get 2 for the price of 1! But it can be incredibly powerful when the people in your network share something extremely special about you.

Fifteen years ago I moved to a new state and didn't know a soul. I was hired to start a business from the ground up. Within less than a year, my office became one of the most profitable branches in the company primarily through cold calls. I did approximately sixty-five face-to-face, nose-to-nose, toe-to-toe cold calls every single week... and then I was introduced to referral marketing.

Within six months, the referral group I participated in generated over half of my revenue. Referral marketing didn't change my bottom line. My bottom line was just fine! It changed the way I hit my bottom line. I didn't have time for cold calls. I got walked past gatekeepers and straight to decision-makers by people who were willing to lend me their credibility. Getting referred to prospective clients shortened my sales cycle, increased my closing ratio and changed the way that I did business forever.

So when I was offered the opportunity to make referral marketing MY business, I said YES. Now my day, every day, is about helping people experience those same kinds of results by building strong, active networks. In one year alone, my local clients passed over 19,000 referrals that resulted in over $10 million dollars. Local referrals... local dollars... local businesses!

That's my story. What's yours?

Your story is like a snowflake, one of a kind. It's exclusively yours. It may be the only thing that truly separates you from the rest. When my referral partners find themselves standing in the middle of a referral and share my story, they begin to separate me from my true and perceived competition by answering one of the hardest questions we all have to answer. Of all the people who do what you do... what's so special about you?

MOTIVATE IT!

All right, close your eyes and picture all of the people that you know standing around you. I mean ALL of them! This is your network. Many of them know you, like you, trust you and understand what you do... so why won't they refer you?

They have their own lives to live and their own businesses to build. After all, time is a limited resource. Why should they leverage their most precious resource for you? The fact of the matter is that different people have different motivators. It's up to you to figure out what inspires each and every person in your network so they will actively listen and take action on your behalf.

Sound impossible? It's not. Dr. Ivan Misner is known as the "Godfather of Modern Networking." He says that a good networker has two ears, one mouth and uses them proportionately. Bottom line... you've got to LISTEN! You must be present in every conversation.

There were two things that I absolutely adored growing up – ballet and Bon Jovi – and there was one young man that was bound and determined to give them to me. He joined a ballet guild so he could surprise me with tickets to see Swan Lake. Then I found myself front row center at a Bon Jovi concert. Jon Bon Jovi tossed the hat from his head straight to us while singing *Livin On A Prayer*. I still have the hat. My 15-year-old son has staked his claim on it.

Those things didn't just cost money. They required time, effort, energy and persistence. He had to do some fact-finding, take time off work, inconvenience co-workers, stand in some long lines and probably take a lot of grief from his friends for the whole ballet thing.

These days, I do a lot of speaking so I get some really great gift baskets. The most common item included in each basket... chocolate. One of the things I dislike most on earth... chocolate. I know, I know, I'm officially out of the girl's club. I just don't like it!

Getting chocolate or receiving some random white wine instead of my favorite red doesn't demotivate me. I really do believe it's the thought that counts. It simply tells me that they haven't taken the time to get to know me.

How is it that a teenager can instinctively know that you need to get acquainted with someone and do the necessary "work" to build a relationship, but grown business professionals seem to think it will happen naturally?

If you want to build long term, reciprocal relationships with the people in your network, you've got to figure out what they really, really want and then do your best to help make it happen. Maybe they'd like you to sponsor an event; volunteer at their favorite non-profit fundraiser or they just need your advice in a particular area. The easiest way to figure it out is to offer those five magic words – How Can I Help You? *Then stop talking and listen!*

ACTIVATE IT!

Testing your network means you're testing your relationships. It can be very scary and incredibly revealing!

You want someone to endorse your products or services... when was the last time you endorsed theirs? You want a referral... when was the last time you referred them? The real question is: How do you know that you've done enough to earn the right to ask anyone for anything? ...Tracking!

I learned the hard way that even when it feels like you're doing all the right things to earn referrals from your network, tracking makes sure that you know the truth by showing you your actual results.

In the beginning I literally tracked everything – every person I met and every move I made. It was a huge time investment, but what I learned was priceless! Relate2Profit.com, my CRM (Contact Relationship Management) software of choice, told me that I was working wide, but not deep. I was purposefully connecting a lot of people, which meant I was making a lot of people a lot of money. But they were one-sided relationships, so I was building everyone else's business but mine.

So I decided to limit the majority of my giving (and tracking) activities to a handful of my closest colleagues. Without a doubt, these were people I could count on to refer me. I called my top five newly identified referral sources my Fabulous Five. Relate2Profit soon told me that they weren't the right five people. While I did a whole lot of giving to them, I didn't even get 5 referrals out of the whole bunch.

I was beginning to feel defeated. I help people build strong, active, profitable networks for a living, so why can't I put together my own referral network? Once again, tracking gave me the answer because I finally had enough data to see who my referrals were consistently coming from, and the giving activities that motivated them to proactively refer me.

I am finally working with the right people. It takes a lot less time, effort and energy to maintain my referral relationships because I know which strategies motivate each person based on results. Relate2Profit tells me that I've finally gotten it right and so does my bottom line.

The reality is that you can *build* a network that includes all the right people who are properly *educated* and *motivated* to take *action* on your behalf and it still isn't enough. There are other critical factors that have a huge impact on your referrability. Here are just a few to consider:

REFERRABILITY FACTOR #1:

Specialize. Know one thing and know it well. Make yourself the "go to" person in your market by creating success and becoming a true expert in your industry.

REFERRABILITY FACTOR #2:

Follow up and follow through. Be responsible and accountable. Don't just tell me what you're going to do. Actually do it and do it well… because so few people do.

REFERRABILITY FACTOR #3:

Demonstrate your depth of knowledge. It's extremely easy to refer to someone that can undeniably prove they know their business inside and out through words and deeds. You better be at the top of your game if you want the opportunity to serve the needs of the people in my network!

Is referral marketing common sense? Yes! Well then, why aren't there more billionaires walking the Earth? Because "it may be common sense but it is not common practice." (*Steven Gaffney, Author of Just Be Honest – Authentic Communication...*). I also learned from the best in this business that success is often found in the uncommon application of common knowledge (*Dr. Ivan Misner*). So maybe it's not rocket science, but referral marketing is a science, nonetheless, that must be learned and applied.

Coming from such a long line of successful entrepreneurs that started their businesses from the ground up, there was never any doubt that I'd start my own business. It's in my blood. It was a matter of finding something that I loved enough to make it my life's work. I found a true love for referral marketing and I firmly believe it is the "thing" that I was put on this earth to do, because I'm not just building my own business. My day, every day, is about helping future generations make their business dreams a reality by *building their own ultimate networks.*

ABOUT PAULA

Paula Frazier is an internationally recognized referral marketing expert with over a decade of experience in helping people build powerful personal networks that produce high quality referrals. In just one year, she helped hundreds of business professionals throughout Southwestern Virginia pass along over 19,000 referrals that resulted in over $10 million dollars in transactions.

Paula is honored to be one of six elite Master Trainers for Referral Institute®, an international referral training and consulting company. She is also a long time Executive Director for BNI®, the world's leading business networking organization. Paula is acknowledged as a true leader in her industry and has been awarded for her achievements in market penetration, program development and mentoring.

Paula's networking articles are regularly featured online. She has contributed to books such as THE Book On Business from A to Z, Brainsbook on Networking and is also acknowledged in the New York Times Bestseller, Truth or Delusion—Busting Networking's Biggest Myths.

Paula lives in the beautiful Blue Ridge Mountains with her husband, Neal, and their teenage children, Neale and Griffin. She considers her family to be one of her greatest successes.

Citing the uncommon application of common knowledge as her key to success, Paula is a fourth-generation entrepreneur who has traversed the highs and lows of business ownership and has grown intimately familiar with the risks, rewards, challenges, and excitement of starting business ventures from the ground up.

Because of her passion as a small business advocate, Paula's day...every day... is dedicated to helping future generations make their business dreams a reality.

CHAPTER 13

FROM NOBODY TO SOMEBODY:

HOW TO QUICKLY, EASILY & STRATEGICALLY CREATE A PERSONAL BRAND ONLINE IN 9 EASY STEPS

BY MICHELLE VILLALOBOS

MY (SHORT-LIVED) CAREER AS A "NOBODY"

I started my sales and marketing consulting business several years ago after leaving the magazine publishing world. From the beginning I knew I'd have to network to generate business, and early on I had a networking experience that changed the direction of my business – and my life.

I met a "hot" prospect at a Chamber networking event who was interested in working with me after we had a great conversation about marketing and sales. Unfortunately, when I caught up with him a few days later, he confessed that he had done some homework. He had "Googled" me and found... nothing at all. That worried him, because he said he wanted to go with someone "more established."

So I went online and Googled myself. Sure enough, that first page was filled with results for "Michelle Villalobos" - only one of whom was even me. Who knew there were so many people with my name out there? In fact, the only result that was actually mine was from back when I was still in the magazine business.

That situation was a wake-up call. I realized I had work to do.

THE IMPORTANCE OF BEING A "SOMEBODY"

Fast-forward four years. These days, when you Google my name, you find literally thousands of results for me (and more every day), web search results, image results, video results and more, all of which tell the story of who I am, what I do, and the value I deliver.

Now, most of our leads are generated online – a combination of people meeting me in person then looking me up online, and now even people finding me online before they ever meet me in person!

Getting to this point was no accident. I carefully researched, planned and executed a strategy to raise my profile and build my reputation online. Creating a personal brand online has become an essential component of my in-person networking efforts.

Surprisingly, however, I constantly meet people who (a) don't realize the importance of branding themselves – not their business, but them, the *person* – and (b) think it's a lot harder to do than it really is.

GOOGLE IS THE NEW RESUME

If you're actively networking to generate business, chances are the prospects you meet are going to research you online to decide if you're trustworthy, credible and someone with whom they want to work.

So, when people look for you online, what do they see?

When they Google you, friend you on Facebook or look you up on LinkedIn, does what pops up represent you well? Is your personal brand consistent across platforms? Does it tell the right "story" about you?

We've all heard at least one nightmare story of "that guy" who lost his dream job because of that inappropriate photo on Facebook, or of some crazy college night coming back to haunt some girl we know... But what about the more subtle damage when your online reputation simply doesn't measure up to what people expect?

The most valuable asset you own in business is your reputation. And these days, your online results *are* your reputation (or at least a huge chunk of it). From your search results to your Facebook page to the recommendations on your LinkedIn profile, *Google is the new resume.*

GETTING REAL ABOUT YOUR ONLINE BRAND

It's no longer about *what* you know, or even about *who* you know. It's about *who knows YOU* - and what they think you can do for them.

Having a strong online presence that represents you well is one of the most fundamental strategies you can undertake to make your networking more effective. At the VERY least you must "own" that first page of Google search results.

So what does it take? The good news is that it's a lot easier than most people think. It's not rocket science, but it does require patience, focus and dedication.

Here are the nine fundamental steps to "owning your name" online and branding yourself in a way that supports your in-person networking efforts. Some of these tactics you can complete in a few minutes, and see big results right away. Others take more time, and the benefits may take a while to reveal themselves.

But if you do this, I promise you, it will make a big difference.

1. DEFINE YOUR BRAND

Define your personal brand as narrowly as you can. Consider these essential elements:

- What value do you provide (rather than what services do you offer)? Here's an example, if you are a personal trainer, try positioning yourself in terms of the result: "lose weight," "get in shape," or "get hot." Keep in mind that to cut through the clutter, you'll want to choose something memorable, something "sticky." David Barton Gym uses "Look Better Naked." Now that's memorable.

- Who is your target customer? Get specific. If you say "everyone" or "anyone," that's simply not defined enough – especially online.
- In what geographic area do you focus?
- What makes you different from your competition (your USP - unique selling proposition)? This is a tough one because a UNIQUE selling proposition by definition means that other people can't say the same thing. So if you say "unparalleled service" or "top-notch quality" that's simply not unique enough (because everyone says that). How are you *truly* different from everyone else? That's your USP.
- What are some basic key words (like "luxury real estate" or "small business coach") that you'd like associated with your name?
- What do you want to be "top of mind" for?
- From the above, create a one-liner that describes who you are and what you do, that you can start using in multiple places (more on where to deploy this later). For example, mine is: *"Michelle Villalobos delivers never-boring workshops, seminars and keynotes to help professionals – especially women – market, sell and promote themselves. Our programs are 100% performance guaranteed, or you don't pay."*

Keep in mind that your goal is ultimately to be "top of mind" for something, and it's impossible to be "top of mind" for multiple things – at least at first. So if you have a side business or have two jobs, you need to choose one brand that encompasses both, or just focus on one.

2. ESTABLISH A BASELINE & SET UP ALERTS

First things first: do a Google search of yourself (put quotes around your name) and see how many results come up. Take a screen shot of your web results, as well as your image results and video results (top left corner of your Google results page). Do this now, before implementing the rest of these strategies, and then periodically (i.e., every month, quarter, year), to see how far you've come.

Next, set up a Google Alert (www.Google.com/alerts) for your name. This way you'll be the first to know when Google comes across your name on any websites, for example, in media stories, online reviews, blog posts, even comment boxes on certain sites. This is highly addictive, you'll love seeing how often your name starts to show up on the Internet once you implement the tactics here.

As you become familiar with alerts, you might want to add more – for your brand, for your competitors, for clients, for industry keywords, etc.

3. OWN YOUR NAME

Go buy your URL. You can go to www.GoDaddy.com (or a zillion other options) and purchase yourname.com. For example I own www.MichelleVillalobos.com. You can redirect that URL to point anywhere (like the "About Me" or "About Us" page of your company website). If you don't have a website, for example, or you are an employee, you can redirect it to your LinkedIn profile (which we'll get into in a moment).

So what happens if your name is common, or you share your name with a celebrity? Well, you've got your work cut out for you, but it's not an insurmountable problem. Here's what you can do:

- Could you add a middle initial or middle name? Keep in mind that if you do this, you'll really need to use it across all platforms – even when you introduce yourself to people and on your business cards. Think Michael J. Fox - he never goes by Michael Fox because the "J" is part of his brand.
- What about a descriptor or a pseudonym? For example, a colleague of mine, Dr. Mike Woodward, uses "Dr. Woody" professionally. Go ahead - Google him and see how it's worked.
- Follow your name with your keywords or coin a term or phrase. For example, if you brand yourself as "Mary Smith, party planning queen," people will likely remember those keywords when looking for you online.
- Brand yourself geographically, if it makes sense. For example, if you're a real estate agent focused on Miami Beach, FL, use that on everything: "John Meyer, Miami Beach Luxury Real Estate." Keep in mind if you're micro-targeting or trying to go bigger.
- Consider using an alternate spelling of your name. I know

someone with a common name who changed his name from "Marco" to "Marko" and he was easily able to take over his name.

If your name is difficult or complex, that can actually be an asset. For example, my last name "Villalobos" causes all sorts of misspellings and mispronunciations. So as part of my branding I use Michelle Villalobos (vee - ya - low - bos) to draw attention to how it sounds.

4. CLAIM YOUR PROFILES

Now that you've defined your brand and your name, you need to go "claim" it everywhere you can. Certain places get "crawled" by Google more often and more intensely than others, you'll want to start with those. Describe yourself using those key words that you came up with in Step 1. Make the profiles public.

It could take anywhere from a few days to a few months for them all to start popping up high on your Google results.

Here are a few of the best places to start:

- **LinkedIn.com** - be sure that you fully flesh out your profile here and that you review it often because LinkedIn is often the very first result for most people. Getting people to recommend you here is a great idea. Keep in mind that the "Professional Headline" gets crawled, so put the phrase you came up with in Step 1 into this box.
- **Google Profiles** - obviously Google crawls it's own content, so this is an easy way to get a quick result. Go to www.Profiles.Google.com to fill yours out.
- **Google Maps** - If you have a physical location, this is a great way to generate visibility. Go to google.com/maps and follow the directions to "add a listing." Then ask clients and friends to post reviews. It's better if the reviews happen over time, rather than all at once.
- **Plaxo.com**
- **ZoomInfo.com** - ZoomInfo gathers info about people from all over the Internet, and often has erroneous information. You can look yourself up then "claim" and correct your profile.
- **YouTube.com** - Eventually you'll probably want to post video content because guess what? YouTube is the second most

popular search engine after Google. Plan ahead by claiming your profile now.

- **Flickr.com** - Flickr is for posting photos. If you upload photos and tag them with your name, you'll get a search result for each photo you post. Here's a trick: I export all my slideshows as images, then tag each one with my name – voila! several results within a few *days*.

- **Twitter.com** - Even if you do not plan to use Twitter, it can be helpful to set up the profile and seed it with 10 or so tweets that are relevant to you and your brand. Not only does each post provide yet another search result, it looks good to see 10 good, relevant tweets when people click into your profile.

- **Slideshare.com** - Slideshare is especially useful for those of us who do speaking engagements or consult. If you fill out this profile, post at least one slideshow that educates people about your field (*not* a sales pitch or a sales presentation as these won't get much traction). I post all of my slideshows here and have thousands of views and downloads that have delivered speaking leads. Cool bonus: both LinkedIn and Facebook have plug-ins so you can feed your slideshows into them – this is a great feature to help your slideshows "go viral."

All in all: own your name everywhere you can, on all big social media sites – even if you don't plan to use them – so no one *else* can claim them.

5. ESTABLISH A "HOME BASE"

You should have a presence in one major spot that accurately and fully reflects your brand. Best place: your own website or blog. If you don't have either, another good choice (for now as a placeholder) is LinkedIn, because it tends to climb to the top of most people's Google results.

Keep in mind that just because you have a blog doesn't mean you have to write all the time. I have clients who hate writing and have video blogs or photo blogs instead. You don't have to write, but you do need to post interesting, entertaining or informative content on a regular basis (Google loves new content).

6. SHOW YOUR FACE!

When meeting you in person, it is said that people make a judgement about you within the first 3 seconds. The same is true online.

Simply put, online pictures and profiles are the new "first impression." For better or worse, how you are perceived visually is just as important as what you can do – at least at first. Plus, people want to do business with people, not with brands, or logos, or companies.

You need at least one *great* picture of yourself, one that is aligned with your brand and your niche. To see some examples of work we've done with clients, you can visit www.HeadshotWorkshop.com.

I am a BIG believer in getting professional portraits shot. All experts have professional portraits, and the best head shots make it clear who they are and what they do. By the way, just because a photo is professional, that doesn't mean it has to be cheesy, fake or boring!

Here are some ideas for planning and choosing a great photo:

- Don't edit while shooting, edit once you're done. Example: I use Sharpies in my workshops to release creative thinking and my purse is always full of at least a handful of colors. So during my photo shoot, I just pulled them out and played around. There were about 100 bad pictures, and one magical one. That photo became a cornerstone of my brand - go ahead, Google me and see for yourself.
- When you do a photo shoot, be open-minded, try everything. You can always trash the photos later. The creative process and the editing process are opposites, don't confuse them! One requires open-mindedness, the other critical thinking.
- Use a current photo. A photo that looks old screams "stuck in the past." Not only is it unprofessional, but you're missing the opportunity to keep your brand as current and as relevant as you are.
- Even if you were more "beautiful" 10 years ago, chances are these last 10 years have given you experience, character and depth. Don't hide that.
- I counsel women to consider avoiding the ever-popular "head tilt." It's a "little girl" pose that can diminish your credibility, particularly in male-dominated fields.
- Eye contact. While some situations/personal brands require

something different, by and large, making eye contact engenders trust. And we all know trust is the basis of every relationship – business or otherwise.

- Use a variety of shots in different places – but keep them looking consistent. One idea: take lots of pictures in the same outfit in several different poses.
- Afterward, pull a handful of images: close-up, medium and full body. You can even use the same photo cropped several ways.
- Be authentic and show your personality! Just because you're getting a professional headshot, doesn't mean that the photo has to be generic, stiff or boring.
- Try to capture what you do somehow – perhaps use a prop or props.
- Retouch and crop strategically. A photo can be transformed with creative cropping and talented retouching.

Whether your brand is "Earth Mother," "Badass Exec," "Girl-Next-Door Entrepreneur," "Marketing Queen," "Trustworthy Financial Planner," "Kooky Artist" or something completely different, a portrait can and should project your unique brand.

7. BECOME THE "VOICE" OF YOUR NICHE

Think of ONE way that you can you deliver value to your target on a regular basis, and in what format:

(1) 1-minute YouTube "how-to" videos?
(2) A blog?
(3) Inspirational quotes?
(4) Twitter?

Only pick what you know your audience/target market/potential clients want. (FYI: they likely DON'T want to know about what you had for breakfast, whether you're stuck in traffic, or if your kids are driving you crazy.)

Regularly send valuable information out into the cyberverse that will appeal to and draw in your narrow target audience.

Tools that you can use: YouTube, SlideShare, Wordpress or Blogger, Flickr, Facebook, Twitter, and more. There are probably dozens of others custom-made for your field.

8. USE EMAIL MARKETING

It is said that the average sale requires 7 touches. I don't have time to contact people individually 7 times after I meet them at a networking event. If it weren't for my email marketing, my "warm" prospects would quickly cool and fall through the cracks.

So what I do is send out valuable info that my audience wants on a regular basis via email. Email marketing is easy, inexpensive and can be very effective (assuming you send out really good material).

When I bring up email marketing, I invariably get asked about spam. No one wants to be a spammer - and no one wants to receive spam (even though we all do).

How can you avoid being spam? Well first and foremost, you need permission to send email. How? If you meet someone in person, ask them! I have yet to be told no, once I describe what I send. Another way is to use a subscription box on your website and other places where people can sign up.

Second, you need to make sure people can unsubscribe from your list. I use Constant Contact email marketing so that I don't have to micromanage this process.

And third, on a qualitative level, send great content! Figure out what your ideal target audience wants, and send it to them on a regular basis. I am subscribed to several emails that I hungrily await (like www.tut.com's daily "Notes From The Universe" and the three-times-a-day HARO - "Help A Reporter Out"). Why? Because they deliver true value to me.

Think of it this way: If they don't LOVE it, its just spam (it's so true that we even named one of our workshops this title!)

9. BE ACTIVE, CONSISTENT AND PATIENT.

How long do you REALLY think it should take? Triple that. Just kidding. Actually, I'm only half kidding. The fact is that some of these steps will work quickly, like magic, others – like email marketing – may take more time to work. But put altogether they represent the best and easiest tactics that I've used for myself and with clients to build powerful online reputations.

I'll leave you with a quote from my hero in personal branding, Gary Vaynerchuk. This is from his book <u>Crush It</u>:

"Mark my words, if you want to stay relevant and competitive in the coming years – I don't care if you're in sales, tech, finance, publishing, journalism, event planning, business development, retail, service, you name it – you will still need to develop and grow your personal brand. Everyone – EVERYONE – needs to start thinking of themselves as a brand. It is no longer an option; it is a necessity."

ADDITIONAL RESOURCES:

Visit www.MakeThemBeg.com to get great (free) strategies on personal branding. On that site you can also enroll in a Training Program called *Make Them Beg: How To Stop Selling & Start Seducing With Your Irresistible Personal Brand*, which I developed together with Jessica Kizorek, founder of www.BadassBusinessWomen.org.

You can also find several free resources at my website: www.MichelleVillalobos.com, including:

- *Stop Drowning In Business Cards*
- *It's Not Who You Know... It's Who Knows You*
- *101 Power Networking Tips, Tricks & Techniques*
- *The Perfect 10 In Sales: The First 10 Seconds, The Next 10 Minutes & 10 Days Later*

ABOUT MICHELLE

MICHELLE VILLALOBOS has developed thirteen programs that have collectively been delivered – either virtually or in person – to over 70,000 people. She teaches, trains and talks about personal branding, networking, referral marketing, and the unique challenges women face in business – like "How To Communicate Powerfully (Without Being A Bit%$)."

The *Miami Herald* named Michelle one of its annual "20 Under 40" in 2011. Michelle's blog is featured on the website for Lifetime TV's show "The Balancing Act," and Telemundo regularly brings Michelle in to discuss how to get ahead in business. Michelle is bilingual and Hispanic.

As an entrepreneur, Michelle has launched numerous endeavors. One of the most successful is *The Women's Success Summit*, featuring hundreds of attendees, speakers, and sponsors. The event is currently Miami's largest business conference for women, and expanding to several other cities nationwide. In addition, Michelle's client roster features names you'll recognize. For example, she has delivered her trademark "never-boring" programs for Burger King Corporation, Gibraltar Private Bank & Trust, Frito-Lay and Lexis-Nexis.

Michelle advocates an "anti-marketing" approach to business, one that eschews traditional "push" tactics in favor of "pull" strategies that draw referrals, opportunities, media exposure, and – ultimately – sales. This is what she teaches clients, both individual and corporate.

Michelle's speaking style is casual and fun, and she regularly busts out her rainbow assortment of Sharpies to illustrate points using everyday, audience-appropriate examples (she recently constructed a price-value matrix using her shoe collection – the audience loved it).

Michelle holds an undergraduate degree from Dartmouth College in Psychology modified with Mathematics, and an MBA in international business from University Of Miami. She is also qualified to administer and interpret the Myers-Briggs Personality Inventory (MBTI) and loves all manner of personality tests, quizzes and books. She is an ENFP, by the way.

Michelle's latest training program, "Make Them Beg" (www.MakeThemBeg.com) (developed together with Jessica Kizorek, founder of BadassBusinessWomen.org) is a wake-up call to anyone who still thinks that business success is still about "selling" instead of "seducing" or that Google *isn't* the new resume.

Michelle's loftier mission in life is to eradicate gossip, backstabbing and unhealthy competition among professional women so that they can "get along, get ahead and get promoted." To this end she recently published "Why Women Play Dirty" (www.WhyWomenPlayDirty) to raise awareness about this controversial and oft-avoided topic.

Since Day One Michelle has offered a no-holds-barred, no-questions-asked, no-excuses performance guarantee with every program, speaking engagement or product she delivers.

CHAPTER 14

PREDICTABLE RELATIONSHIP DEVELOPMENT

BY BRAD LEPPLA

Like anything of excellence or value in life, constructing, nurturing and leveraging a successful network can represent a significant investment in time and effort. Creating shortcuts to mitigate the significance of the investment involved exposes the effort to unproductive risk that can result in disappointment, time wasted and ultimate failure. While it is true that one can build a successful network of referral sources through shortcuts (cold calling, for example), the process can be decidedly unpredictable.

Careful, predictable development and nurturing of relationships is vital to the successful networker. To best leverage any and all opportunities available, it makes sense to develop an effective network of referral sources and collaborators in a predictable and focused fashion. The risk-laden relationship needs to be identified quickly and, if resurrection is possible, a plan is required to guide one around the obstacles presented (creating the means to gain the end). Having no plan or creating shortcuts indicates too much focus is directed towards short-term gains (achieving the end justifies sacrificing some of the means). The successful network-er will be a keen observer, have the ability to react to changing condi-tions, and understand how best to apply certain principles and guidelines in order to make his/her networking efforts successful.

Among the myriad resources available to the networker, two well-documented tools will be used in this chapter to help guide the proper and efficient development of the networking relationship. Alone, these tools provide a basic foundation for understanding human relationships. Combined, they provide a strategic roadmap to successfully navigate the relationship-development process.

VCP MODEL*

This model describes the stages through which any *successful* relation-ship (personal, professional, or otherwise) *must* evolve.

All relationships start at the **Visibility** stage: the participants in the newly forming relationship become aware of one another and the prod-ucts and services offered by each. It's fairly obvious, if I am to form a relationship with you, I need to know you exist. If I am to buy your products, I have to know they exist. One cannot graduate to the next stage, **Credibility**, without passing through Visibility first. As the rela-tionships are strengthened through continuous, positive reinforcement (actions, testimonials, and products), the increase in *mutual* trust and credibility propel the relationship upward. The final stage, **Profitability**, is gained when the relationship has achieved *mutual* implicit trust.

The Credibility and Profitability stages must have *mutual* agreement among participants insofar as correct placement of their relationship in the VCP Model is concerned. Otherwise, a complete breakdown of communication and relationship-building can (and will) ensue. Imagine, for example, the difficulties created as one person perceives their relationship exists in the Profitability stage while the other participant sees the relationship in the Visibility stage. *Ever been to a networking event where one person is attempting to sell something to another person they have just been introduced to?*

DISC MODEL**

Each person is wired in such a way that their *perception of their environment* (task-oriented or people-oriented) drives what *actions they will take in response* (outgoing or reserved). As a result, there are four different types of observable behavior that give us an "objective and descriptive 'language' for thinking about our attitudes and actions."

D – stands for **Dominance**, Outgoing/Task-oriented

> Self-starters, in-control leaders, make quick decisions, demanding, decisive, determined

I – stands for **Influence**, Outgoing/People-oriented

> Fun, friendly, center of attention, carefree, persuasive, impressionable

S – stands for **Steadiness**, Reserved/People-oriented

> Predictable, stable, team player, warm-hearted, patient, harmonious

C – stands for **Compliance**, Reserved/Task-oriented

> Cautious, analytical, procedural, slow decision-maker, value-oriented, courteous

Everyone is a unique blend of these four parts. However, we must also be aware that personality styles expressed (and perceived by others) depend upon our *interpretation of the appropriate responses required* to influences from our environment. Therefore, a "natural" style is an expression of how our brains are wired naturally (behaviors that are comfortable to us), while an "adaptive" style is how people adjust their DISC traits in order to succeed (how much a natural style is masked in order to fit in).

PUTTING IT ALL TOGETHER: THE ROADMAP

Combining these two models gives us a multi-dimensional method for interpreting perceptions, then advising appropriate re-actions (if necessary) in the building of successful relationships.

	V	C	P
D	Confidence	Non-competitor	Added Value
I	Smile	Warmth / Substance	Reliability
S	Listen	Supportive	Team-player
C	Quality / Excellence	Consistency	Trust

Adaptive ——————————→ Natural

Interpretation: It is your perception that I am a "D". In the beginning stages of our relationship development (Visibility) you will want me to see you as a confident, self-assured person if the relationship is to be given a chance to proceed further. This might very well be an adaptive style for you! To advance into the Credibility stage I must see you as a non-competitor (in other words, you will want me to perceive that you are not challenging my authority or trying to outdo my "D"). To get to the Profitability stage of our relationship you will want me to see you as someone who consistently adds value to our relationship.

To explain it a little differently, let's take a look at how each personality style might describe a flower:

D – It's a flower (short, to the point, no amplifying information needed)

I – It's sweet-smelling with rich, vibrant yellows and blues (warm, full of life, creates an image)

S – It's beautiful (descriptive of a feeling)

C – It's a 6" green stem that is 1/8" in diameter terminating in a 3" yellow head with blue, paper-like, oblong petals radiating from the center… (exacting language).

In possession of this flower over time, a "D" might recognize his/her changing perception of the flower:

Visibility – It's a flower
Credibility – It's a valuable flower
Profitability – It's indispensible to me

As relationships progress towards the Profitability stage, there might be less of a tendency to rely upon adaptive styles, as there is a corresponding increase in trust and credibility. The differences between natural and adaptive styles likewise become more visible, acceptable, and potentially less important in the relationship-building process. Trust builds tolerance and understanding.

How do we know when we are dealing with an adaptive style?

1. Ask leading questions: Family, Occupation, Recreation, and Motivators (what motivates you to excel?).
2. Lots of talk (adaptive style), different action (natural style).

Sometimes we have no choice but to respond appropriately to the *perceived* style until progress through the VCP Model is sufficient to reveal the natural style.

NAVIGATION

A person's willingness and ability to recognize changing conditions then respond accordingly is critical to the successful development of a relationship (or correct identification of a potentially risky relationship that should be avoided). Those unable, or unwilling, to identify and conform (in other words to navigate the roadmap) will find themselves able to develop relationships only in very narrowly defined niches of their own choosing (sometimes unintentional). For example, a die-hard "D" may see no value in commencing a relationship with an "I" perceived to be "flighty and unfocused." Similarly, a "live-life-to-its-fullest", fun-loving "I" may not be interested in understanding the "arrogance" of a "D". These relationships probably have little chance, if any, of progressing beyond the Visibility stage – until both parties are willing to take a risk at learning and adapting.

Finding a relationship partner who shares an interest in building and developing a relationship for long-term mutual benefit will facilitate successful, predictable and efficient navigation of the roadmap. Both of you will give and get the clues that will continually drive the relationship to the Profitability stage. The journey may start at the S-V box (I will listen attentively to you), shift over to the C-C box as I pick up clues that guide me to your natural style, and end up at the C-P box where I have performed in such a manner as to cause you to develop strong trust in me. Remember, perceptions represent reality… until proven otherwise. Pay close attention to the clues.

AN ILLUSTRATIVE STORY

Tom is a high "I" and believes he is a master networker. Based on several recent collaborations with Bill, Tom believes their relationship exists in the Profitability stage and sees Bill as a high "D". There is a marketing seminar that Tom believes will be very beneficial to Bill's business, and wants to invite him to attend.

He approaches Bill as a perceived "D" in the Profitable stage and states, "Bill, I need you to go to this seminar with me tomorrow. It will help grow your business and has done wonders for me. What time shall I pick you up?"

Unfortunately for Tom, Bill's natural style is "C" and he perceives his relationship with Tom is barely in the Credibility stage. Sensing correctly that Tom is an "I", Bill amicably reminds Tom that more information about the seminar is required in addition to more timely notification.

Since Tom is an otherwise astute person, he perceives the need and desire for reevaluating his assessment of Bill to determine an appropriate new course of action. Consequently, Tom will adapt and learn how to successfully navigate his relationship with Bill. With Bill's assistance, patience and understanding of the roadmap, the relationship can develop along a predictable, albeit non-linear, path to success.

---

* *Business By Referral: A Sure-Fire Way to Generate New Business* by Dr. Ivan Misner Ph.D. & Robert Davis, p. 36 – 38.

** *Getting to Know You* by Chris Carey, p. 9 – 10

ABOUT BRAD

Brad Leppla, Chief Operating Officer and one of four Executive Directors for Business Network International (BNI) of Colorado & Southeast Wyoming, originally hails from the San Francisco Bay Area in California.

Brad graduated from the University of California, Berkeley with a Bachelors degree in Forestry. He joined the U.S. Navy shortly thereafter to fly jets. He trained in the A-6E Intruder carrier-based bomber and flew 44 combat missions over Iraq during Operation Desert Storm in 1991.

Retired from the Navy in 1998, Brad started his own Information Technology company, and joined BNI as a member in 2001 to grow his business. An avid history buff, Brad has participated for almost 20 years as a Civil War re-enactor, regaling many a campfire with his banjo playing. He resides in Colorado Springs, Colorado with his wife of 24 years and their three children.

CHAPTER 15

THE NETWORKING DISCONNECT

BY DR. IVAN MISNER

I was at a networking event in Europe a few years ago where more than 500 people were in attendance. The speaker who was on stage just prior to my presentation asked the audience: *"How many of you came here hoping to do some business today–maybe even make a sale?"* The overwhelming majority of the people in the audience raised their hands. He then asked, *"How many of you are here hoping to buy something today?"* **No one raised a hand—not one single person!**

This is the networking disconnect.

If you are going to networking events hoping to sell something, you are dreaming. Do not confuse direct selling with networking. Effective networking is about developing relationships. I know, I know. . . there is always someone out there who says, *"But, Ivan, I've made a sale by attending a networking event!"* Okay . . . I am not saying it doesn't *ever* happen—it does. I am just saying it happens about as often as a solar eclipse. Face it, there are times when even a blind squirrel can find a nut. Any businessperson can stumble on some business at a networking meeting from time to time. However, when you have most of the people at an event trying to sell something, and virtually no one there to buy something, you are crazy if you think the odds are in your favor to "sell" at a networking event.

So why go to a networking meeting? You go because networking is more about farming than it is about hunting. It is about developing relationships with other business professionals. It is not about 'direct selling.' This means you need to move the relationship through the VCP Process®. This is a chronological process that begins with Visibility. This stage is where people know who you are and what you do. Visibility leads to Credibility where people know who you are, what you do – and they have learned that you are good at it. Credibility then leads to Profitability. This is where people know who you are, what you do, they know you are good at it and they are willing to pass you referrals on an ongoing basis. The VCP Process is the foundation of any successful business networking effort.

With many people, there seems to be a significant disconnect between intent and reality relating to their expectations at a networking event. This kind of disconnect leads to poor results, which then leads people to exclaim that "networking doesn't work." Well, from what I've experienced myself over the past the past three decades, along with the results I've witnessed with hundreds of thousands of people around the world – networking works just fine. However, one's intention must be in alignment with the reality of the particular circumstances. If nobody at an event is looking to buy something and you are there trying to sell something – you have a disconnect. If you are there to meet people and move through the relationship or VCP Process, then your intention and the reality of the situation are more likely to be in alignment.

Sometimes you go to a networking event to increase your visibility and to connect with people you have never met, sometimes you go to establish further credibility with people you know, and sometimes you may even go to meet a long-time referral partner and do some business. In any case, the true **master** networkers know that networking events are about moving through the relationship process and not just about closing deals.

I had someone recently say to me, *"I'm still amazed at the number of people I run into at networking events that still don't understand it's not a sales event, it's a networking event! They come to the event, try to sell, don't get any sales, and then they're disappointed!"*

Another person told me that *"There is a great opportunity to be found in connecting with people and getting to know them. We need to start seeing each other as interesting human beings as opposed to a potential sale!"*

I find it ironic that so many people are disconnected relating to a process that is supposed to be all about becoming connected.

There is a paradigm shift that needs to take place before you can make your networking efforts work. That shift is to move from a 'direct sales' mentality to a 'relationship networking' mentality. If you go to networking events looking to meet new people and move through the relationship process with people that you meet and get to know, then you are working the process correctly.

Here are five things to remember when attending networking events:

1. Don't go there to sell, go there to connect.
2. Have some meaningful conversations with people you meet.
3. Follow up with people you found interesting or who you can help in some way. Don't follow up to sell them something.
4. Meet these people in a one-to-one setting, learn more about them, and ask them: *"how can I help you?"*
5. Go for the long-term relationship, not the short sale.

Remember, networking is more about *farming than it is about hunting*. So, the next time you go to a networking meeting, think about how many people are there to 'buy' something. Then, remember to stop 'selling' and start networking.

ABOUT IVAN

Dr. Ivan Misner is the Founder & Chairman of BNI (*www.bni.com*), the world's largest business networking organization. BNI was founded in 1985. The organization now has over 6,000 chapters throughout every populated continent of the world. Last year alone, BNI generated 6.5 million referrals resulting in $2.8 billion dollars worth of business for its members.

Dr. Misner's Ph.D. is from the University of Southern California. He is a *New York Times* Bestselling author who has written over 12 books, including his latest one, called *Networking Like a Pro,* which can be viewed at: *www.IvanMisner.com*. He is a monthly columnist for Entrepreneur.com and is the Senior Partner for the Referral Institute – an international referral training company *(www.referralinstitute.com),* with trainers around the world. In addition, he has taught business management and social capital courses at several universities throughout the United States.

Called the *"Father of Modern Networking"* by CNN and the *"Networking Guru"* by Entrepreneur magazine, Dr. Misner is considered to be one of the world's leading experts on business networking, and has been a keynote speaker for major corporations and associations throughout the world. He has been featured in *The L.A. Times, The Wall Street Journal,* and *The New York Times,* as well as numerous TV and radio shows, including *CNN, CNBC,* and the *BBC* in London.

Dr. Misner is on the Board of Trustees for the University of LaVerne, CA. He is also the Founder of the BNI-Misner Charitable Foundation and was recently named *"Humanitarian of the Year"* by a Southern California newspaper.

He is married and lives with his wife Elisabeth and their three children in Claremont, CA. *In his spare time (!!!),* he is also an amateur magician and has a black belt in karate.

CHAPTER 16

3 STEPS TO PROFITABILITY FROM RELATIONSHIP MARKETING

BY ELAYNE LIEBERMAN

In today's high tech world of internet marketing, electronic books, e-cards and technical devices, it's easy to forget the significance of face-to-face, personal touch relationship marketing. If your database of potential and actual clients and customers combines both high-tech and personal touch, then you are covering your bases and leveraging multiple tools to grow your business and reach true profitability.

Internet Marketing and Relationship Marketing are necessarily interconnected. It's all about relationships. And building relationships on the internet is really no different than building them in your community, face-to-face.

So let's talk about Relationship Marketing with that crucial personal touch, and three powerful steps to building your business by gathering a strong database established through trust and confidence.

STEP 1:
THE REALITY OF BEING VISIBLE

Do you remember when you started your business? You were excited. You felt like your product or service was so totally amazing that everyone would immediately come flocking to you. You knew about customer service because you knew how you liked to be treated as a customer. You established your business goals and set financial targets for the next 12 months, two years, five years and beyond.

You thought to yourself, "Oh boy, oh boy! This is gonna be great! The money will just come flowing in and I'll be able to retire in 10 years."

Perhaps you attended a Chamber of Commerce mixer and handed out your business cards left and right, telling everyone you approached about your business. You thought that because *you* knew you were trustworthy, that everyone would automatically trust you. You might also have built a website and started rudimentary internet marketing.

Back at the office you waited for calls and orders to come pouring in. And you waited and waited. You called several of the people you met at the last business mixer to set up an appointment, but they didn't return your call or didn't have time to make an appointment with you. And while they were polite, you could feel their disinterest. Perhaps this puzzled you.

You waited some more, hoping something would happen from all your hard work at the networking event. At the next business mixer you diligently talked to everyone, "networking", telling them about your business and handing each person a card. You felt that surely, this time the phone would start ringing.

"I just haven't met the right people," you told yourself. You still imagined all the money you'd be depositing in the weeks ahead. And you waited and waited, but no one called.

Now you've begun to think that business networking, and perhaps even internet marketing, simply isn't the right way to market your particular business – or, worse yet, it's too hard to do. There's too much to learn and it feels overwhelming.

But did you ever ask yourself why it wasn't working? Why weren't people calling you? Could you figure out the answer? Most of us can't understand why, when we've met someone and given an outstanding explanation of our services or products, why in the world those people won't contact us or do business with us. It's a mystery!

Well, actually, it's really no mystery. There's a simple explanation why this rarely works.

Imagine for a moment that you're at a business networking event. Someone you've never met comes up to you and starts talking non-stop about his business and how incredible his products are and how much he loves what he does. You stand there, nodding your head and hear yourself saying, "Ah Huhm. Yah. Nice." …while you continue to nod your head to pretend you're interested in what this guy is saying. In reality, you're bored out of your mind and you have absolutely no interest in this guy or his business. He's coming on too strong and it feels pushy to you. All you want is an excuse to get away. You're just trying to be pleasant and courteous. The guy hands you his business card and you can tell he's all excited and has no idea you're not interested. Not once has he asked about you or what you do, what your interests or needs are. He has no idea if his products or services will help you or not. He hasn't asked any questions to find out! He has no clue. But, guaranteed, he'll expect you to be calling him soon. And if he doesn't hear from you, you can be sure he'll be calling you.

Think about this. You've just met this guy. You don't have any real idea who he is. You haven't even begun to establish a relationship with him. He might appear to be a nice person, but how can you know? He might be trustworthy, but how do you know for sure? He might be a true expert in his field, but you have no evidence of this because you just met him. It takes time to know what someone is really like, right? And right off the bat, he's come on so strong, that you feel yourself taking a mental step or two back and away from him.

Now think about your past experiences at those Chamber mixers. With which person do you relate? …The listener or the talker?

Just because you attend business mixers and events and you meet the same people there again and again, doesn't mean that you've established relationships with them. You are probably visible to them. They recognize you and say hello. But, so far, that's as far as it's gone. The same is true of internet marketing. You may have an incredible website, filled with information. But information alone isn't enough. It's the relationships you build, whether on the internet or in person, that hold the key to building credibility and reaching profitability.

Let's say you speak with this guy on the phone about his products and services as well as yours. Now you're both initially informed about one another. But you haven't developed a meaningful relationship with each another. However, you've possibly started one. Over time, you may communicate more and maybe you even observed him conducting business with others. But you're both still just in the Visibility Stage with one another.

So just being visible doesn't get you the business. But it is a very important step because it sets both of you up to be instantly recognized and for others to be aware of you and your business. You want to become very visible. You want to be recognized. And you have to keep working at staying visible.

As you become more visible, you can start learning more about others, who they are, what they need, what they are looking for in their personal and business life. The more you know about others, the more effective you'll be as a valuable Referral Partner to other business professionals; the more valuable you'll be as someone who can fulfill a need and solve problems: the more likely you will earn referrals as time goes by.

You can't jump from visibility right into profitability in one easy step. Human nature simply won't let that happen because we're wired to protect ourselves and the people we care about.

So visibility is just the first step in the process of becoming profitable. At this stage, you simply become aware of one another and the *potential* as a source of referrals for one another or the *potential* as a customer. Actively working to become and remain visible is crucial to moving to the next step of credibility.

STEP 2:
CREDIBILITY IS A STEPPING STONE TO PROFITABILITY

Time has now passed. You've been to more business mixers and you've spoken with a number of people with whom you've become acquainted over the past year or so. You now start to have expectations of one another. You expect follow up and follow through with what they say they'll do. You expect professionalism. You expect stellar customer service. You expect integrity. You expect reliability and confidentiality. You expect fair prices in exchange for products and services.

And they expect the same from you.

Once those expectations, both implicit and explicit, are fulfilled time and again, you've reached the point where credibility buds.

Once each of you feels confident in the other, and both of you are satisfied with the relationship, then it will continue to grow and strengthen into one of deep credibility and trust. Appointments are kept and everyone shows up at the agreed upon time. Results are proof positive.

But how can you know for sure if someone is credible? How can others know if you are credible? Usually people ask other people what they know. Questions like: Have you done business with this person? What was your experience? Do you know of others who have done business with him? Did you get what you paid for? Was she honest with you? Do you trust his advice? Was she fair? Did he listen to what your needs were?

Third party testimonials and verification are smart business practices. Think about it. If you refer a business colleague to a friend or associate, your reputation is on the line – every time. And when they refer to you, their reputation is on the line. In the past, I've referred business people to friends and family based simply on what others have told me and their visibility to me. The results were sometimes less than acceptable. So I recommend that you do your own research. Privately ask more than one person, perhaps two or three, and possibly use the service yourself before recommending that person and business to others.

Again, it takes time to build credibility. Be patient. Use the time wisely. Continue attending business networking events and maintaining your visibility. Make appointments to meet one-on-one with other business professionals to learn about their business and what kind of a person they are. Ask their permission to add them to your electronic database and send them your e-newsletters and other internet marketing materials.

Meet one-on-one with your current clients or customers. Establish a personal relationship with as many people you already do business with as possible. Once they feel they can trust you and have confidence in you, they will begin referring the people they know, like and trust to you. And your database grows and your credibility in the eyes of others gets stronger. You know the old saying, "Your reputation precedes you." Make sure that reputation is the one you want!

The amount of time it takes to reach credibility in the minds of others is often dependent on the type of business you're in. Some professions, by their very nature, require more time to reach credibility. Are you willing to hand over the investing of your retirement portfolio to just anyone? Are you willing to let just any dentist drill holes in your teeth? What about hiring an attorney to represent you? I'd want to be sure I was hiring the right person for the job, and someone on whom I could count in the most difficult of situations. What is the level of risk you'd be taking by hiring this person?

If I were planning a birthday party and wanted flowers and cake, I would probably ask around to find out what other people's experiences and recommendations were, in hiring and working with, a florist and a bakery. I would go and taste the cake and take a look at the flower arrangements available. It wouldn't take too long to make a decision. The time factor is much shorter in this case because I wouldn't have high financial or legal issues or my health at stake. So, for the florist and the baker, it would take less time to build to the stage of credibility.

At long last, you've reached a point in your marketing process where you are credible in the eyes of fellow business professionals, as well as clients, friends and family. That's great. You're getting some personal business from them and even the occasional referral to others outside that 'circle of influence.' You're starting to generate an income that pays the bills and gives you some take home pay.

STEP 3:
PROFITABILITY IS NOW RIGHT AROUND THE CORNER

You've now developed relationships beyond visibility. You continue nurturing those relationships and developing new ones. Your reputation in the community is solid and you are recognized as a knowledgeable professional in your field and are a contributing member of the business community. Your credibility is growing and more and more people are using your services. You are referring business to others, as well. Yes, you are generating an income stream and you are delighted.

But the real question is, are you profitable?

Let's define profitability. <u>The American Heritage Dictionary</u> defines profit in the following ways:

1. The return on investment.
2. The return received on a business undertaking after all operating expenses have been met.
3. An advantageous gain or return.
4. The amount received for a commodity or service in excess of the original cost.

Being profitable, by this definition, infers that you are receiving an advantageous gain and return on the investment of *your* time, *your* money, *your* effort and *your* energy. But let's explore this a little further.

What if we added *leverage* into the mix? Leverage of other people's time, effort and energy? Wouldn't that tend to create even more results than from your efforts alone?

So let's expand the definition of profitability.

Profitability is an advantageous gain and return on investment from your time, money, effort and energy, *as well as that of others*.

Okay, so you're generating an income from your marketing efforts and you're getting some business from your business associates, clients, friends and relatives. These are called Tier 1 Referrals. But are these folks sending you new business by referring others to you (Tier 2 Referrals)? And if so, are those referrals sending you referrals (Tier 3 Referrals)?

Solid profitability comes from Tiers 2 and 3 and beyond. Your business keeps growing from word of mouth referrals and marketing.

Visibility comes from patience and continuously exposing yourself and your business to the people with whom you want to do business.

Credibility comes from establishing yourself as an expert, someone who is trustworthy and goes beyond what's expected.

Profitability comes from cultivating relationships, trust, dependability and integrity, and that usually takes time.

It doesn't have to take forever to go from visibility to credibility and finally into profitability, if both people are growing and nurturing the relationship. Remember, you are investing in yourself and your business every time you reach out and touch someone – face-to-face!

ABOUT ELAYNE

Elayne Lieberman is a Master Results Coach. In business as a health and wellness consultant and coach for over 30 years, Elayne realized the power and intelligence of Relationship Marketing early on. She now specializes in assisting small business owners to reach success with proven Relationship Marketing techniques.

Elayne and her husband Steve opened and ran a delightful, successful and well-loved specialty bookstore in Old Town Eureka, California, called White Dolphin. Customers signed up and received a monthly newsletter written by Elayne, and invitations to lectures, book signings and performances held in the store. It was wildly popular and great fun.

In the early 1970's, Elayne stepped into the world of Network Marketing and fell in love. Her success in the industry is based on her ability to understand human nature; the workings of the mind and heart, as well as the deep need for personal touch. Today, she teaches, trains and coaches network marketers and other business professionals how to generate sales outside their warm market, preserving their treasured relationships with friends and family. Her forthcoming book, *The ABCs of Relationship Marketing*, targeted specifically to the Network Marketing Industry, will be the perfect guide to success for every network marketer, whether new to the industry, or a tried and true MLMer.

Elayne is an Area Director for BNI, Business Network International, in Ventura County, California. As such, she teaches, coaches and trains BNI chapter members how to maximize their results from their BNI experience, give and receive more referrals and enjoy more closed sales.

She is certified as a Nutritional Consultant, Hypnotherapist, Reiki Master and as a Results Coach, with a Bachelor of Arts in Psychology from the University of California, Los Angeles.

Visit her blog at: www.ElayneLieberman.com. She can be contacted by email at: Elayne@BNI-VC.com.

CHAPTER 17

THE CREDIBILITY QUADRANT™
– BUILDING SOCIAL CAPITAL THAT LASTS

BY TR GARLAND

"All of us have benefited from the industrial age, the technology age, and most recently, the age of information. And without question, we have entered into the most influential age ... the age of association. Never before has it been more crucial to be connected to, or associated with, people of influence. There is no doubt that the biggest impact to your personal and professional life will be determined by 'who' you are associated with, and your 'connection' to them."
~ *John C. Maxwell*

THE POWER OF ONE MAN'S NETWORK

For most American schoolchildren, the name Paul Revere often conjures up legendary images of historic proportion. You see, as the story is told, Revere was the messenger who rode horseback from Boston one brisk, pre-dawn morning in April 1775 to deliver an important warning to the surrounding communities that the *'red coats were coming.'*

By the time the British soldiers had mobilized toward Lexington that very same day, the colonial resistance was already well organized and in place. As a result, the British were soundly beaten at Concord, giving rise to what history would later record as the **American Revolution**.

While the result of Paul Revere's ride may be history, let's take a little closer look at the actual sequence of events which may shed some light into the true value of 'building social capital.'

On that unforgettable night, two different men rode two different routes from outside Boston to Lexington, warning communities along the way of the imminent threat from the British. The message delivered by Paul Revere and William Dawes on their midnight rides was critical to the outcome of events that would unfold. It informed the recipients that the very next morning the British army intended to march on Lexington to arrest colonial leaders, and then, to aggravate the situation, on to Concord to seize colonial guns and ammunition.

What makes this conversation intriguing is that both Revere and Dawes carried the <u>identical</u> message through just as many towns over just as many miles. Whereas Revere's message spread like wildfire in the New England communities, Dawes' message failed to ignite any form of interest. The result was that in towns he was responsible for informing, even the local militia leaders weren't aware of the British plan of action.

Why was there a difference in the reception of this identical message?

Evidence suggests that Revere was connected to an extensive network of strategic relationships, whereas the points of contact for Dawes were, to be quite frank, less useful.

Here's an account from Malcolm Gladwell's -*The Tipping Point*:

> *"In two hours, Paul Revere covered thirteen miles. In every town he passed through along the way – Charlestown, Medford, North Cambridge, Menotomy – he knocked on doors and spread the word, telling local colonial leaders of the oncoming British, and telling them to spread the word to others. Church bells started ringing. Drums started beating. The news spread like a virus, as those*

informed by Paul Revere sent out riders of their own, until alarms were going off throughout the entire region. Paul Revere's ride is perhaps the most famous historical example of a word-of-mouth epidemic."

This account of Paul Revere's ride provides a noteworthy example of the power and effectiveness of building the ultimate network, and the social capital that comes with it. It also includes many of the ingredients essential to introducing you to some foundational concepts of business networking that, if applied correctly, can assist YOU in building YOUR ultimate network!

THE SAME STORY THROUGH A DIFFERENT LENS

Now that we've got a vivid picture in our mind's eye of the legendary and impactful role of Paul Revere, let's look at the history books through the eyes of the Referral Institute and how it applies to word-of-mouth marketing today.

More specifically, let's look at this story through the lens of the VCP Process®.

We're going to drill a bit deeper and actually dissect the actions of Revere that resulted in changing the world's political, economic, and geographical landscape forever. (Think about it. If Revere didn't succeed, we might all be speaking with an English accent. Wouldn't we?).

First, let's revisit the <u>VCP Process®</u> to networking.

It focuses on the methods of creating, growing, and strengthening business relationships that evolve over time. It's a chronological process that must be adhered to, and is useful for assessing the status of a relationship and what *stage* one is at, as it pertains to the referral process.

'V' STANDS FOR VISIBILITY.

It's where people know who you are and what you do.

When one invests the time to look deeper at the history books, what's found clearly backs up the necessity of 'Visibility' as a foundation. David Hackett Fischer recounts in his book ***Paul Revere's Ride***: ***"The silversmith was one of the relatively few mechanics in the top echelons***

*of the Boston Whigs. He had attended strategy meetings, engraved po-
litical cartoons, hosted the first commemoration of the Boston Massa-
cre, served on town committees, and joined in the Boston Tea Party."*

In short, Revere was highly visible (and subsequently highly connected), due to his frequent societal activities.

The key here is that to be an effective networker, 'Visibility' must be
actively maintained and developed; without it, you cannot move on to
the next stage.

'C' STANDS FOR CREDIBILITY.

It's where people know who you are, what you do, and that you're good at it.

Gladwell explains that one reason Revere's ride was so effective was
that it was Revere himself who made that ride, and not someone else.
He was a world-class networker. People knew him and he knew people.
When Revere spread the news, it wasn't a stranger spreading that news,
but a person they knew, recognized, and trusted. He had 'Credibility'.

So when Revere banged on doors and shouted, he didn't have to explain who he was. The trust he had built over decades took care of that.

'P' STANDS FOR PROFITABILITY.

*It's where people know who you are, what you do, that you're good at
it...and they're willing to give you referrals back and forth on a reciprocal basis.*

For the sake of this comparison, 'Profitability' could be explained as
people taking action on your behalf. Revere is believed to have trig-
gered the actions of as many as 40 additional riders who traveled
throughout the surrounding areas to spread the news.

History paints a clear picture that Revere's Visibility led to his Credibility, which in turn, led to Profitability.

A FOURTH LETTER TO THE PROCESS?

It's important to note that there are only 3 letters in the VCP Process®.
So, one would assume there are only 3 steps to the process, right?

For the sake of conversation, let's introduce another letter into the mix.

Let's propose that we place the letter 'I' just before the letter 'V' which helps describe the sometimes uncomfortable situation called 'In-Visibility'. It's when you haven't made a big enough impression with people you meet while networking, for them to remember who you are 30 days from now.

To tie this back to our history lesson, William Dawes certainly fell into the realm of 'In-Visibility'. Historians find it unthinkable that he spoke to no one along his assigned path. And, because there is almost no record of anyone who remembers him that night, he simply had not built up the Visibility and Credibility that Revere had done over time.

Sure, he may have met people beyond Boston at some point previously. But, he never made an impression. And, the reverse is probably true too, as it appears Dawes didn't know whom he should be waking up.

Just like Dawes, why would you invest the time networking if no one is going to remember you?

A BUSINESS PHILOSOPHY IN TUNE WITH TODAY

There is a clear shift in society today. As a result, businesses must adapt not out of choice, but out of necessity. If they don't, they'll be left behind. Their revenues would begin to dry up in a matter of months, because they would've lost connection with their target market and their target market with them.

It's apparent that there's a massive swing away from the *me, me, me* viewpoint and towards a much more civic, harmonious, and "can't we all just get along" community belief system.

If this is happening to business in general, wouldn't it make sense to apply this insight to your networking efforts?

The Credibility Quadrant™ is a foundational business philosophy that consists of 4 Core Components that, if applied correctly, will help you successfully navigate through the VCP Process® to networking – all the way to Profitability. It's the most applicable and relevant approach to building Social Capital today.

All components are mandatory. Not one of them is optional. And, much like the <u>VCP Process</u>®, it is chronological – in a counterclockwise fashion.

CORE COMPONENT #1 – INTENTIONS

The scandals that have become prevalent over the last decade have caused a strong distrust for Corporate America and any marketing message they employ.

As a result, people (i.e. your target market) have a sense for anything without positive intentions. They're more apt to rely on product recommendations from their peers than any manufactured message. This is seen in the meteoric rise of popularity in websites such as Yelp and Foursquare (and to some extent, aspects of Facebook, Twitter, and even LinkedIn).

Did anyone ever question Revere's intentions? No. He had plenty of chances for people to see him and get to know him so that his intentions were always transparent.

In order to bring history's lessons into modern day and more specifically into relevance for you and your Business Networking efforts, it's suggested you consider the following questions:

<u>**Qualifying question/s:**</u>

1. What are your intentions (for joining a networking group or entering into a business relationship)?
   - Are they visible, hidden, or even mixed messages?
2. Why do you want to meet a particular someone?
   - Can you help them? Or can they help you?
   - Do you have mutual friends or interests?
   - Do you want to sell them something?

Be aware that sometimes when you're in roles of increased 'Visibility' your 'Intentions' are clearer and even amplified – which is not always a good thing. In other words, your true colors shine through.

Sometimes, people shift into what's considered to be 'Visibility'-overload. Every chance they get, they're doing "stuff" to be visible without having any sort of 'thought out' strategy. And, sometimes this ends up backfiring and ultimately defeating the overall objective of networking to build trust and credibility. After all, perception IS reality!

CORE COMPONENT #2 – CONTRIBUTIONS

Revere knew everyone and had an "uncanny genius for being at the center of events," according to David Hackett Fischer. He goes on to state:

> *"When Boston imported its first streetlights in 1774, Paul Revere was asked to serve on the committee that made the arrangement. When the Boston market required regulation, Paul Revere was appointed its clerk. After the Revolution, in a time of epidemics, he was chosen health officer of Boston, and coroner of Suffolk County…As poverty became a growing problem in the new republic, he called the meeting that organized the Massachusetts Charitable Mechanic Association, and was elected its first president…"*

I trust that you get the picture. Revere was someone whose contributions were well documented.

Whereas, Dawes escaped being captured by the British, but doesn't seem to have taken advantage of this to contribute anything more. In contrast, Revere kept working after he was captured and released. According to reports, he got Hancock and Adams away from Lexington, went back to hide Hancock's papers, and finally days later, sat in on the Patriot leaders' next strategy meeting.

<u>**Qualifying question/s**</u>:

1. What contributions are you making to your network and business relationships?

Truth be told, many people get into the Credibility Quadrant™ (that is moving from 'Visibility' into 'Credibility') by exemplifying the first 2 Core Components of positive 'Intentions' and making consistent 'Contributions'. But, they never get out.

It takes a true skill to get unstuck and move into 'Profitability'. Understanding behavioral styles is what is often overlooked by most networkers.

CORE COMPONENT #3 – RELATIONSHIP INTELLIGENCE

We're all familiar with the Golden Rule, which is simply *"treat others as you wish to be treated"*. But in networking, Dr. Tony Alessandra's much-heralded **Platinum Rule** is what the elite practice. In short, it's *"treat others as they wish to be treated"*.

The application can be broken into 3 steps:

1. Understand your own Behavior Style
2. Understand that there are other Behavioral Styles out there
3. Understand how to identify and adapt to those other Behavioral Styles

This type of relationship intelligence was certainly applied by Paul Revere. Was his approach in the delivery of his message the same with each person he addressed? Absolutely not. There is no doubt Revere knew that he needed to adapt and how to adapt.

If this approach produced results for Revere, shouldn't you consider adapting your message depending on whom you're networking with?

<u>Qualifying question/s</u>:

1. What is your Behavioral Style?
2. What is the Behavioral Style of people you do business with?
3. What is the Behavioral Style of people you WANT to do business with?

CORE COMPONENT #4 – TRAINING

When surveyed and asked the first thing that comes to mind when they hear the word "Training", professionals report that they think of their schooling, on-the-job instruction, and even their continued accreditation.

However, when discussing the Credibility Quadrant™, these forms carry considerably less weight as compared to the "training" that one's own journey through life has provided them.

You see, each person has very unique life experiences that help mold them into who they are. Embrace those lessons that life has taught you, and use them to offer the marketplace something unique – something only you can offer.

Today's focus is on the *"You Economy"*. So, networking and the trust you build from it should be about *"You"*. If you understand why it's recommended to place more importance on this point, then you will dramatically increase your chances of navigating through the last of the 4 Core Components – and finally enter 'Profitability' in your networking relationships.

Qualifying question/s:

1. What lessons has life taught you (good or bad)?
2. How can you use these lessons to offer the marketplace something unique?

THE NETWORKING DISCONNECT

It takes years of networking, being visible and building credibility, to have the kind of impact that Paul Revere had. I'm puzzled then when people think they can get immediate results from *their* networking efforts.

Most people view networking as the "art" of passing out business cards and shaking hands with possible prospects. Evidence can be seen in your own local community by the surge in popularity and buzz around events that claim to be your community's biggest mixer. But, truly what they have been calling "networking" is actually "selling". Isn't it?

Networking, or at least how the experts view it, is more about identifying potential business partners with whom we can be building long-term relationships with. So many people focus solely on finding prospects versus having formal Referral Partners bring prospects to them.

When people join a strong-contact network such as BNI or even a casual-contact network like a local Chamber of Commerce and expect immediate results, their mindset isn't in the right place. This is why using the VCP Process® and the 4 Core Components to the Credibility Quadrant™ as a foundation to your networking efforts is so important. It separates the novices from the professionals and creates an ROI that lasts a lifetime.

Why network if you cannot raise your "stock value" enough to build trust and credibility with others in hopes that they will refer someone in their network (time and again) to do business with you?

YOUR REPUTATION AS CURRENCY

The actions you take and the relationships you develop create a foundation

for Social Capital. Your reputation – where you are in the <u>VCP Process</u>®
and whether or not you've successfully navigated through the Credibility
Quadrant™ - directly affects your influence in your local community.

Paul Revere made an impact and changed the events of history. Wouldn't
it make sense then to learn from the aforementioned examples and apply them if you want to make a similar impact within your network?

Never lose sight that not only was Revere's approach applied to business
(networking), it was also his approach to life in general. Social Capital
stems from people's perception of you as a person; it gives you access to,
and influence upon, your network. And, one of these days, you are going
to need people to listen to what you have to say. You're going to need to
ask people for that introduction to someone in their network. And if you
haven't built up enough capital, your transaction will get declined.

Think about it. You are a financial institution - a bank *per se*. Every interaction with your network is an investment (a deposit to or a withdrawal
from); so choose your investments wisely. And, maybe, just maybe you
can build an ultimate network that would parallel Paul Revere.

*"From the minute I first met TR, he started doing what he does best
– offering creative ideas, tapping into his resources, and making
connections to those in his network – and he hasn't stopped yet. TR is a
dazzling combination of big picture vision and non-stop action!"*

-Libby Gill, Business Coach, Brand Strategist & Bestselling Author of
"You Unstuck"

Bibliography/Works Cited:

I wanted to make a special note to thank those whose works have influenced my life, education, and writing
style on the topics of Business Networking, Referral Marketing, and Social Capital. Some have influenced
the above content more directly than others, but I want to give credit nonetheless:

"An Executive's Primer on the Strategy of Social Networks" 2009 by Mason A. Carpenter for the historical
concept behind the first segment of my chapter.
"Paul Revere's Ride" 1995 by David Hackett Fischer
"The Tipping Point" 2002 by Malcolm Gladwell
Multiple blog posts from Brian Solis
John C. Maxwell
Dr. Tony Alessandra
Numerous conversations with my fellow Referral Institute colleagues
And too many conversations and written work to list from my mentor, Dr. Ivan Misner
VCP Process® is a registered trademark of the Referral Institute and is used with permission.

ABOUT TR

TR Garland (www.TRGarland.com) has achieved levels of personal & professional prosperity that others only dream of. And his mission is to help those in his network accomplish the same – because, quite frankly, he admits to being a "Habitual Giver."

In fact, he is the recipient of Bob Burg's prestigious *"Go-Giver Award"* which recognized him as a shining example of **The 5 Laws of Stratospheric Success – Value, Compensation, Influence, Authenticity, & Receptivity.** This award was presented to him by Dr. Ivan Misner himself.

TR's Sphere of Influence ranges from his local community of Orange County, CA and spans internationally. His network consists of A-Lists as well as Up & Coming Speakers, Authors, Thought Leaders, and Internet Entrepreneurs.

He is being mentored by such world-renowned names as Dr. Ivan Misner, who **CNN** calls *"The Father of Modern Networking"*, Michael E. Gerber, author of **"The E- Myth"** book series who **Inc. Magazine** calls *"The World's #1 Small Business Guru"*, and legendary Personal and Professional Development Expert, Brian Tracy.

As a result, many consider him one of today's leading authorities on **Business Networking**, **Referral Marketing**, and **Building Social Capital** (that lasts a lifetime). Through the Referral Institute®, TR is a consultant to top performers & entrepreneurs on creating a sustainable business plan based on strategic and effective business networking. He guides people to create and maintain deeper business relationships that build stronger bonds, which ultimately create "Referrals For Life®".

TR's advice has been featured in many local publications, but also nationwide publications such as Entrepreneur Media/Magazine.

Testimonials for TR Garland

"I have been at the forefront of the world of business networking for over two decades and among the many people I've come into contact with, few possess as great an understanding of the nuances of both online and offline networking as TR Garland."
~ Dr. Ivan Misner, NY Times Best-Selling Author, Founder of BNI

"When you have an opportunity to sit with TR, look into his eyes, and feel his sincerity and passion for helping others, it's no wonder why many (including me) consider him one of the leading experts on building Social Capital."
~ Michael E. Gerber, Best-Selling Author of The E-Myth book series

"I've known TR for years and not many people are better poised to teach you about how Business Networking has traditionally been conducted and how it's going to be conducted in the future than him. He's a true authority on the subject."
~ Brian Tracy, Best-Selling Author and creator of "The Psychology of Achievement"

"TR Garland has a unique ability to develop a plan of "how–to's" for reaching your vision. His commitment is unwavering and gives 110% to those of us he assists. It's a pleasure to work with him."
~ Susan RoAne, Best-Selling Author of "How To Work A Room"

"From the minute I first met TR, he started doing what he does best – offering creative ideas, tapping into his resources, and making connections to those in his network – and he hasn't stopped yet. TR is a dazzling combination of big picture vision and non-stop action!"
**~ Libby Gill, Business Coach, Brand Strategist &
Best-Selling Author of "You Unstuck"**

"Dr. Ivan Misner and TR Garland are two people who I not only consider Business Networking Experts, but who I consider knowledgeable enough to understand that your behavioral style affects your 'Referability'. Their insight could be the difference between success or failure in your networking efforts."

~ Dr. Tony Alessandra, Best-Selling Author of "The Platinum Rule" and "Charisma"

CHAPTER 18

BUILDING THE ULTIMATE NETWORK...

USING "MAGIC WORDS"

BY TODD DELMAY - THE NET LEARNING CENTER

s human beings, we use the spoken word to communicate with others in ways that the written word simply cannot convey. Tone, inflection, and volume are just some of the elements that add to, or take away from, the impact our words have on a listener. But the exact words that are chosen have just as much importance, and can often mean the difference between getting what you want, and getting nothing. *Words Matter.*

I've held a theory for a long time that in most situations, especially where you want something, it is critical to know the "Magic Words" that will get you what you want or need. Beyond "please" and "thank-you" – or even "open sesame" – though these words can all be defined as effective means for bringing about a desired result.

In business, we know that some people are simply more successful than others in getting what they want out of life and business. So what are the secrets that they practice to select and then weave the right words into story form? And how can you find the right words to do the same thing?

Most people think they know how to talk about themselves and their business, but it is only by choosing carefully the right Magic Words, and then building them into stories, introductions, and conversations we use everyday, that we will connect, relate, and invest in the relationships and networks around us.

Many years ago, I was on a flight back from London on British Airways. After the drinks service, I saw the flight attendants coming down the aisle to collect "used service items" (three words that lack magic). One of them seemed to be frustrated, moving very slowly along, trying to get the attention of everyone in his section one at a time. I noticed he was naming all of the things he was collecting: "Cups? Newspapers? Magazines? Napkins?" etc. And of course nobody was paying any attention to him, which just frustrated him more. Meanwhile, on the other aisle another attendant had figured out that she only needed two Magic Words to get exactly what she wanted – and fast! Aware that she had both British and American passengers onboard, and to avoid any confusion as to what she was collecting, she would humorously turn back and forth to the passengers, first saying in a beautiful, lilting accent for the English passengers "rubbish?" And then turning to say in a nasally American accent, with a very long 'a'- "traaash?" No matter who you were, you knew exactly what she was doing, and it caused passengers to sit up, pay attention, laugh, and poke their seat-mates so they could hear and laugh too, and then get her exactly what she needed.

So where do you find the Magic Words you need to <u>build your Network</u>?

LISTENING FOR MAGIC WORDS

While most everyone can easily be coaxed into talking about themselves, few understand the relationship of the individual words they use to best connect with the listener in ways that resonate. Just because you know your business, doesn't mean you know how to talk about it in ways that are effective. I learn the most by listening to what others are saying, and see how it impacts me. So start listening to what others are saying, whether in person or on the phone. Listen for words that make you think, or feel something. Listen with your heart and well as with your mind, as words that transcend conversation and make you empathize with the speaker have more power.

Depending on how well you know the person, and if you have to first pass through shared experiences (small talk) such as the weather, sports, current events, etc., the dialogue will eventually open up and bridge to a conversation where your Magic Words can break free and achieve your success.

CHOOSING MAGIC WORDS

Choosing your Magic Words is an art requiring patience, persistence, and of course, practice. Whatever Words you choose, they should always fit into at least one quality listed below, although you might not choose to use Words for each quality. Here are the top seven qualities to consider:

1. Human
2. Real
3. Specific
4. Open
5. Humorous
6. Truthful
7. Results

HUMAN (#1)

People do business with people, and your Magic Words should humanize who you are, what your values represent and what it is like to know you as a person. Building a Network is done piece-by-piece, person-by-person, name-by-name, and by finding the right fit with other human beings. We are all tribal connectors seeking out other values-minded humans with whom we can share business and personal interests, and who will be **knowledgeable guides** along the way. Knowing what others truly want, such as your **insider expertise** - and being able to deliver on it - demonstrates that you are people-centered, and that you are worthy of being connected to others.

REAL (#2)

Use words that come from everyday language, not a technical manual. And stay away from words you use daily as a professional, which may

have no meaning for people outside of your profession. Also avoid em-
ulating something you are not by using the business world's most fash-
ionable $100 buzz words (*"used service items"* anyone?). Be yourself,
and passionately present the uniqueness of your brand with words that
fit you, and they will know you are for real.

SPECIFIC (#3)

Too often, business professionals misunderstand what it means to be
specific, and get into a lot of details about themselves, their product,
their service, or their business – that are irrelevant to the listener. Too
many, or the wrong specifics will just put people to sleep (*Cups? Newspapers? Magazines? Napkins?*). In a 140-character Twitter-ized society like ours, it is important to stay focused and use specific words that
make things immediate, and not somewhere off in the out-of-focus distance. The priorities you name clearly define the specifics of what you
have to offer, what you want out of your relationships, and how you're
going to get where you're going.

OPEN (#4)

Not to be confused as the opposite of "Specific", because being open is
about avoiding words that are closed to other points of view, or alternate outcomes. Instead, use inclusive language that allows for people to
see your point of view, and choose to believe you. For example, avoid
the language of absolutes, which can alienate the listener, as people do
not *always* need or want what you're selling, and not everyone *must*
become connected to you. Your listener does not *have* to do anything,
especially if they don't sense you are open to other outcomes.

HUMOROUS (#5)

You don't have to be a joke-teller or a back-slapper, but words can also
be fun, or funny, if used correctly. Remember my flight attendant? We
were all in on "the joke" simply because she chose funny words, combined with the way she said them, to make us laugh and connect with
her. Keep in mind though, that being able to provide witty commentary
or the right amount of levity is good for getting your foot in the door of
a relationship, but staying in takes more depth and substance.

TRUTHFUL (#6)

Nobody likes a liar, and nobody likes the feeling that they aren't getting the whole truth about something either. What you don't say can be as telling as what you do, so always bring the truth with you. If there are natural objections, or widely-held misconceptions about your industry, or company, being truthful and addressing them with honesty and directness makes it far more likely that someone will be willing to listen, and perhaps give you, your company or your product or service, another chance. Especially if it is delivered in a genuine way that is truthful to how you actually feel about what you are saying, the Magic of your words comes through, and can persuade the listener to set aside fear and aspire to go with you where they would **otherwise be reluctant to go independently**.

RESULTS (#7)

Words that convey the **comfort** and **ease** of the result of your product or service, or being connected to you are some of the most powerful. Solutions-based Magic Words convey the attributes to get past the "so what?" question from hearing you simply provide a laundry list of things you "do". And by using future-forward words, and facts, you will lead others to join you on the journey. People don't want to hear what "*might*" be – they want to know what "*will*" be, with some certainty.

TELLING A MAGIC STORY

Once you have listed your Magic Words, putting them into sound-bites and story form will give you things to say no matter how much or how little time you have in a conversation, as well as the answer to almost any question you are asked about yourself or your business. Practicing them so they become part of you ensures the authenticity of deeper Magic.

After college, I worked for a company called Tauck Tours (now called Tauck World Discovery), whose story is a good demonstration of the power of Magic Words fueling a unique success. Woven into a compelling story, they tell of the origins of the company and its set of values, which are repeated after every tour, by every tour director, in every destination. See if you can recognize some of the same words and characteristics I've already highlighted, in the following story.

In 1924, a 26-year-old entrepreneur, Arthur Tauck, was selling aluminum coin trays to banks throughout New England. He was surprised to notice on a beautiful fall day that there were no leisure visitors enjoying the scenery, as few outsiders knew the area well enough to travel through it without guidance.

Since he possessed the insider expertise to show people the beauty of the New England he'd discovered on his travels, and knew all of the locals necessary for creating superior guest experiences at every stop, he could get vacationers to sign on with him as a knowledgeable guide. He would provide for their comfort, while showing them the sights on beautiful back roads that they would otherwise be reluctant to travel independently.

From his first "Tauck Tour" (*a six-day, 1,100 mile, all-inclusive trip in a rented Studebaker that cost his six passengers $69 each*), his original six passengers prompted nearly 20 inquiries about future trips through word of mouth. From there Tauck World Discovery has built itself into the world's leading escorted travel operator, *which has never had to advertise to the public.*

Tauck's signature-style of traveling was developed and refined by providing authentic, engaging discovery of the areas they visit. A friendly, knowledgeable guide highlights the sights and places along the way, while providing in-depth insights into local culture, history, flora, fauna and more. And the trips combine the indulgence of the finest hotels and superior dining, with the ease and assurance of knowing that a professional tour director reliably handles all the mundane chores of travel.

Even from this abbreviated version of the story, you can easily pick out how the Words embody everything Magic about their success, and have most of the seven qualities outlined. Tauck trips could easily be mislabeled as nothing more than "Bus Tours" if told incorrectly, which more often than not are seen as "herding tourists" around like cattle - images and words with which they would never want to associate. Instead they ably redefine travel on their own terms and give the listener a sense of the company's core set of values, its family roots, and the humanity that instantly connects them with their ideal customers – by spelling out the specific results of a vacationers dream only they can fulfill.

By listening for the Magic Words that make you pay attention to others, and by carefully crafting your own set of Magic Words that captivate and move people, you too will have the ability to craft everything from simple sentences to detail-filled conversations, … to presentations that inspire. Over time, your consistent application of your chosen words will become familiar to those around you, and they too will use the words you use, adding fuel to the fires of your future successes.

ABOUT TODD

Todd Delmay is a sought-after public speaker and business coach who teaches entrepreneurs, business owners and leaders how to develop successful stories that sell – by paying attention to using the right language that is specific to the individual or company. Todd's international business experience includes writing and delivering educational programs that bridge understanding and awareness across cultures, businesses and interpersonal relationships. Todd has lead over fifty domestic and international trips designed to give participants a better sense of the world, and the inter-related nature of the global community that now defines the way business is being conducted. He has also produced learning conferences and training programs, which along with his coaching skills, have also earned him recognition for achievements in the field of networking. He has helped countless people discover the power that the spoken language has in getting others to understand them and their business, and to enlist them in supporting their goals. His presentations are valuable, unique, and entertaining.

Todd founded The NET Learning Center as a central point of influential thought and action for sharing the kinds of networking, education, and training that promote business, professional, and personal growth. Drawing from other renowned Contributors in their fields of business success, The NET gives Entrepreneurs, Managers and Leaders the resources to learn (and teach others) the skills, attitudes and techniques they need to succeed in an international, inter-related business environment. Topics such as Leadership, Customer Service, Relationships, Mentoring and a variety of global perspectives come together at the Center of Learning that is The NET.

The NET is a realization of Todd's vision to create a community of business people who are passionate about continuous Education. Its Contributors and Members make The NET more than just a place to learn something from someone else, but a place to also learn by contributing the right information to somebody else to help them succeed. Although there are many places to learn basic business skills, many are asking "what's next?" and The NET has set out to fill that void. Combined with a culture focused on the power of *Mentoring*, The NET offers a dimension of engaging with others that makes information and ideas flow in all directions. The NET is a flexible alternative to a more formal, pre-defined learning curriculum.

Through sharing and empowering each other, a variety of conversations are able to reach the modern businessperson at the individual, team, organizational and corporate level. Members connect via multi-media formats including blogs, podcasts, videos and webinars. But connections and ideas are also put into action offline in face-to-face workshops, seminars, boot camps, business trips and learning conferences.

As a division of the Delmay Corporation, The NET also offers companies and associations the ability to tailor complete programs for their own Conferences, Conventions and Executive Meetings – with certified meeting planners and facilitators who support everything from site selection, to breakout sessions, to keynote speakers.

To learn more about Todd Delmay or The NET Learning Center, as well as how to receive a free copy of their latest special report visit: www.thenetlearningcenter.com or call toll-free (866) 848-5509.

CHAPTER 19

DEVELOP A RESOURCEFUL MINDSET:

USING YOUR NETWORK TO ACHIEVE MAXIMUM RESULTS

BY CHUCK BOYCE

T hroughout this book you will find expert advice on building your own ultimate network of contacts, partners, and resources. The strategies and techniques you learn are of critical importance and have been proven by these experts over many years of practical experience.

As you master these techniques and strategies you will gain the maximum benefit from them when they are applied to your everyday life, those you interact with on a personal level or in a professional setting. To make sure that you are achieving the maximum results of these strategies, you need to consider your mindset when considering the power that is contained within your network.

As a small business coach, I work with plenty of business owners and entrepreneurs that approach each challenge with a resources mindset. They frequently will look at the challenge and immediately bemoan the fact that they could tackle this if they just had more... more money, more time, more help. In the end they are all focused on resources as the solution to the challenge. They are of a resource mindset to problem solving, rather than a *resourcefulness* mindset.

SO WHAT'S THE DIFFERENCE?

The resource mindset leads business owners and entrepreneurs to always be looking for new and more sources of resources. The resourceful minded person will tackle the problem by looking at the resources they have, and who they know that might have access to the resources they need. They look to their network to figure out a solution to the challenge.

This is best illustrated with a classic example. One of the most common challenges for every business owner is the ability to attract more customers in the most cost-effective manner.

A resource-driven business owner will usually look to squeak some money out of his/her budget to put together a marketing campaign. They will pour over the expenses and look for every corner to be cut, and every dollar that can be saved. For the smallest of businesses, it is not uncommon for him/her to actually take the money out of her own salary to fund this activity. He/she is only looking at the challenge from the point of financial resources.

In contrast, if they were of a more resourceful mindset, they would look at the power of the people they know, all of their other resources, and craft a plan to attract more customers using the power of their network. This might take the form of a co-op advertising campaign with a client or supplier that targets the audience. It might be a reciprocal agreement where he/she markets to their partners' customers, and their partners market to his/her customer base.

CAPTURING OPPORTUNITY

In 2008, a longtime virtual office client of the Brandywine Executive Center approached me about expanding their service from just our Delaware location to several other states. We had been working with this client since we opened in 2005. I assured them it would be no problem, as we didn't want to lose their business to someone like Regus, who already had a national presence.

First up, they wanted to add New York, Florida and Pennsylvania. I had just a few weeks to locate service providers, get an agreement in place and start providing the service. I immediately went to my database and looked for people that I knew, knew me, and could trust them to provide this service.

It became immediately evident that I should tap into my relationships in the telemessaging industry. I had working relationships with over a hundred telephone answering service owners in nearly every US state and Canadian Province. These relationships, built up over 5 years of working in that industry, would allow me to fulfill my client's request. Even if I didn't have a contact in a particular state, I was confident that I could use my reputation and the contacts that I did have, to make the connections I needed.

The new partners were happy to take on my client, and for the extra revenue they would receive. My client was pleased that we were able to fulfill his request at a competitive price.

Since we started this expansion, the client has entrusted us with all of their business in the US, and we have partners working with us to provide him with mail-receiving in all fifty states, resulting in a long term, multi-million dollar, multi-year relationship, with a client that started out paying us $400 per month. In addition we have added tens of thousands of dollars in revenue to our partners' businesses.

DEVELOPING A RESOURCEFUL MINDSET

As an entrepreneur, one of my personal touchstones is the advice Bruce Barton, who invented Betty Crocker and gave General Motors and General Electric their names, gave to business leaders, "When you're through changing, you're though." It is important that you continue to work on yourself as well as your business.

If you find that you are presently more prone to the resource mindset, you need to look first at your core beliefs to ensure that they are in line with changing to a resourceful mindset. It is critical that your core beliefs, mindset and actions are congruent. If any one item is out of alignment, it is very similar to wearing a pair of poorly-fitted running shoes. You can probably get to the finish line, but you won't set any speed records, and you will be fighting with pain and discomfort.

Four of my core beliefs that are congruent with my resourceful mindset include:

- I will provide value to others freely without the expectation of anything in return.
- I have the right to ask for help and support from those around me.
- I will respect others decisions not to help and support you.
- I have a duty to use all of the resources within my influence responsibly and efficiently.

All of these beliefs are secondary to, and support my prime belief:

- I have control of my actions, and I accept responsibility for those actions.

Taking control and accepting responsibility allows you to quickly get past the initial reaction to a challenge and move right into problem solving. It may be painful, but by accepting responsibility and taking control, there is always an opportunity to create learning by overcoming the challenge.

Once you have worked on creating the foundation through your core beliefs, the next step is to develop a resourceful mental reflex. Just as we have physical reflexes to certain stimuli, like the smell of a skunk or the heat of a flame, we can develop mental reflexes to words, thoughts and problems.

You can start to develop a resourceful mental reflex, by asking yourself these questions every time you are faced with a new challenge.

- What are all of the resources that I can access?
- Who do I know that can help me with this challenge?
- What value can I provide to them now or in the future?
- How am I going to maximize the benefits received from these resources?

Just as you learned to drive a car, you will need to think about each of the questions very deliberately at first. The process will slowly become engrained, and you will develop an automatic response to a new challenge that follows your resourceful mindset.

All of the work you do to make this mindset shift is going to eventually wither unless you devote yourself to putting it into action. Overtime, you will become less aware that you are using the resourceful mindset, as it becomes the only way you know how to operate.

As you meet new people and make new connections, be mindful of your new resourceful mindset. Approach each new encounter with the thought of what resources you have to share with this person — that will achieve a positive result for both.

ABOUT CHUCK

One of the top alternatives people are using to create wealth in this tough economy is through development of their own small businesses. Chuck Boyce and his organization are helping people do just that by providing online access to resources, while assisting entrepreneurs fight some of the isolation associated with working from home.

"Our goal is to build a community of online resources, so if you find yourself, either by choice or necessity, starting a business of your own, you won't have to figure out everything all by yourself. We have developed a place you can go to get access to the expert information you need. When you have a question, you can ask people who have already faced the problems you're trying to overcome today."

"The current erratic economic situation is what initially inspired us to start this service because we've worked with independent professionals in the past, and saw a growing need for this type of online community to be able to connect people with each other and critical resources. We continue to watch the unemployment rate moving higher, and people are finding themselves unemployed. Thousands of skilled laborers are out of work and many of these people just can't find jobs. Their alternative is to start their own businesses in order to secure their financial future."

Many times, the first thing to be lost after losing a job is a person's self-esteem or self-confidence. Chuck says they offer resources to help people develop the self-assurance they need to start moving forward again. "We try to show them that they are not alone by introducing them to others like themselves that have been in the same situation, have made clear decisions, and moved forward and experienced success in a relatively short period of time."

Tip for Success

"I urge people to set their course and start something new if that is what the situation calls for. I started my own business, a desktop publishing company, when I was 16 years old and have spent the majority of my career working for myself. This is the perfect time to start a small business; in fact, many big companies today had their beginnings during the Great Depression of the 1930's. Small business is what drives our country and you could be a part of that legacy to help the nation return to prosperity. I know that if these potential entrepreneurs give themselves a chance and use our services and resources to build something new, they will also experience the freedom of working for themselves and the financial success we are all looking for today."

If you are interested in learning more go to: http://www.breakingfreeblog.com

CHAPTER 20

HOW TO GROW YOUR NETWORK WHEN YOU HAVE LIMITED CONTACTS

BY SAMANTHA RATHLING

E verything that I am going to share with you in this chapter comes from my personal experience, having built a network from scratch in a brand new country. That network in less than 6 years has enabled my recruitment business to grow from one client and minimal revenue in 2005, to a business which today generates sales in excess of €4.0million. My business now has operations across the UK and Ireland, with in excess of 500 employees. I grew the company through my own ultimate network, but when I relocated to Ireland, where I set up my business, I had no local contacts.

I had previously worked for multinational companies in the UK and The Netherlands. Networking had never been a priority or a necessity, so I didn't have a need to go out and meet people for new business at any stage in my career, because the recruitment company I worked for in Holland was well established, and my role was about account management and not revenue generation. That changed in 2005, when we relocated to Cork. I had two options, work for a local agency, or start my own business. Since the age of 18, I wanted to have my own business, and the timing seemed right, especially since the recruitment market was strong at the time in 2005, when we relocated to Cork.

So in 2005, my company was born. I set up in a very competitive industry, where I had over 80 recruitment agencies to compete with locally. Ireland is a country where EVERYTHING is based on who you know. So who did I know? One person... my husband. I talk in this chapter about growing a network when you have limited contacts, because I literally started from scratch. The good news is that you are probably reading this with slightly more people around you than when I started out.

Whether you know five or five hundred people, the advice in this chapter can be applied at any stage of your business. The more people you know, the easier it will be, but it is not just about adding connections. Understanding relationship-building is vital, and having credibility as a businessperson within your network is the key to making your network work for you. There are eight top tips I am going to share with you.

EIGHT TOP TIPS

N ...NETWORKING GOALS
E ...EDUCATE AND UPSKILL
T ...TIME ALLOCATED TO NETWORKING
W ...WHERE TO FIND NETWORKS THAT WORK FOR YOU
O ...ORGANISE YOUR CONTACTS
R ...REFER AND CONNECT THE PEOPLE IN YOUR NETWORK
K ...KNOW YOUR TARGET MARKET
S ...SAY "THANK YOU"

NETWORKING GOALS

Before you spend any time networking, it is important that you set out what you want to achieve from your efforts. A friend of mine spent hundreds of dollars on attending networking events and conferences, as well as paying for memberships in various networking groups. Although he collected exactly 782 business cards, he received no business. The problem was, he was looking for as many people as possible to sell to, which is how many people approach networking. It is my goal to ensure that this does not happen to you. So what type of goals should you be setting?

- Meet two brand new contacts, and arrange a follow-up meeting
- Meet two new suppliers who can help me
- Make a connection with 5 people in the [XXX] industry
- Find two people who I can give referrals or assistance to

You may notice in my example list, not one of my goals is to buy anything. That's because no one goes out networking with the intention to buy! So why would you want to go out selling? It is much better to focus on making new connections that may be useful to you in the future, or to have the goal to help others.

Often when we network we might meet someone that we know already, which is great if you want to continue to build a relationship with them, but having an existing contact in the room can be distracting. Setting goals for yourself means you are more likely to get what you want from the event by making an effort to talk to brand new people.

I remember the first-ever networking event I attended. I made a connection with a Printer named Patrick. He seemed very friendly and well connected. Within 24 hours of meeting Patrick, he had been in touch with me by email and phone, and had arranged to meet me for a coffee, knowing that I was new to the area. I met him a couple of days later, and he spent over 1 hour learning about my business, finding out more about me as a person, and asking how he could help me. This included the type of clients I was looking for specifically. I actually thought there had to be some kind of catch, especially when I turned to him after an hour and said, so how can I help you? His reply was, "We'll get to me some other time, the purpose of this meeting was for me to help you, don't worry about me." At the time, it was very alien to me, here was a person I had just met, in a brand new town, and he was being so helpful and wanting to help me? It felt very strange!

What Patrick did that week was to give me my first education on how to follow up after a networking event. He also showed me the way to get more business, through giving and helping. Before long Patrick was my Printer and I was passing him business, and after three months he gave me a referral to my first multi-national client. I later learnt that Patrick was a BNI member, and he was the reason I ended up walking through the door of a BNI chapter. I have never looked back.

EDUCATE AND UPSKILL

I am a firm believer that "every day's a school day." Regardless of the type of business you are in, continuous learning and development is essential to success. I have been exposed to some of the best books, audiobooks, podcasts and speakers on networking over the last six years. As soon as I started networking, I learnt the importance of upskilling myself. I attended every training session available, and every relevant national and international conference where fantastic speakers shared their knowledge of networking.

My business coach is one of the worlds leading experts on networking and relationship building, and is a great friend and mentor. Iain gave me a great piece of advice two years ago, which was to spend time in my car listening to audiobooks, rather than music or talk radio. Ever since that day, I have taken his advice, stopped listening to negative news stories, and now feed my brain daily with positive, motivating audio. I listen to at least two audiobooks per week and use my driving time to continually grow my business and lead my fantastic team. This gives me ideas, thinking time and a constant stream of brilliant opportunities to develop new ways of doing things.

I knew absolutely nothing about how to network when I started out; anyone can learn and educate themselves on how to make it happen. Over 90% of my business now comes from recommendations, referrals and repeat business from existing clients. I have become a great networker, with the ability to build fantastic relationships across a vast network of connections, all because I decided to learn how to do it. I have not had to cold-call in over 5 years thanks to my networking efforts, although my industry is notorious for cold-calls. Whether you have a small or large network today, it is never too late to upskill and develop yourself in this area.

The key to my success has been the implementation of great ideas, knowledge and tools to help me grow my business. Networking is a skill and it can be learnt, so it really doesn't matter how much or little you know right now.

TIME ALLOCATED TO NETWORKING

Life gets in the way and despite our best intentions, attending network-ing events can sometimes drop down on the priority list. But when you have a limited network, and you are new to an area, it has to be one of the most important activities for you in your business. Blocking time each week into your diary for networking events and meetings to build relationships, is critical.

In the beginning when I set up my business, I attended four networking events weekly and held at least five one-to-one meetings per week. As follow up after each networking activity is just as important as the time spent at the event itself, I also set time aside to do this.

If 50% of your business comes from referrals and networking, is the time you spend on networking a reflection of this? Is the time you are spending on networking a direct correlation to the amount of business you are generating from your network?

Look at your diary for the last 2 weeks and write down the following:

1. How many networking events did you attend? _____
2. How many one-to-one meetings did you go to with contacts in your network? ____
3. How many hours approximately did you dedicate to networking? _____

This exercise can be very revealing. Based on this 'time-spend' you can now plan to increase or reduce the amount of time you spend net-working, relative to the amount of business you want to receive from networking activities. For example, let's say that you are getting 25% of your business currently from referrals, but you only spend 10% of your time on networking. Imagine how much more business you would generate by word of mouth if you doubled the time you spend develop-ing relationships and growing your network.

WHERE TO FIND NETWORKS THAT WORK FOR YOU

When you have a limited network, it is important to research all of the possible places that you could go networking. The following list is comprised of examples of the types of networks you could tap into:

- Online networks – LinkedIn; Ecademy; Facebook; Twitter.
- Search Engines, search for "Networking Event + [Location]".
- Asking other people you meet, "Where else do you Network?"
- Professional bodies for your industry.
- Your local Chamber of Commerce.
- Women in Business networks.
- Local sports clubs.
- Your children's networks – parents of your children's friends.
- Community Organisations such as Rotary (www.rotary.org).
- Strong contact referral networks such as BNI (www.bni.com).
- Business support programmes in your area.

If you wanted to, you can network anytime, anywhere, online and offline. It is most important that you find networks which work for you. So try as many networks as possible, and see how you feel about each one. What I found useful was to devise a simple scoring system for each network I visited. I scored each event or networking group out of 5, where 1 = poor and 5 = excellent.

NETWORKING SCORESHEET

Was I made to feel welcome?	1 2 3 4 5
Was the event professionally run?	1 2 3 4 5
Did the time and location work for me?	1 2 3 4 5
Did I make any new contacts?	1 2 3 4 5
Does this network have a good reputation?	1 2 3 4 5
Does networking cost anything here?	1 2 3 4 5
What time commitment is involved?	1 2 3 4 5
Will I get business here?	1 2 3 4 5

TOTAL SCORE OUT OF 40: _____

You may find that other questions work better for you, and you can add or subtract from this list, depending on your type of business. The real question is, what will your Return On Investment be? You just have to find the right network(s) for you. Not every network is going to suit your personality, industry, or circumstances. I used to network during the evenings two or three nights per week, however, since becoming a mother of two, these networks are less suitable as I prefer to spend time with my children, so I had to find other networks that fitted with my lifestyle and business needs.

ORGANISE YOUR CONTACTS

Getting organised early is important if you want your network to refer you and generate revenue. When I started to network, I soon realised that keeping on top of my contacts and having a system for my networking efforts was going to be critical. The business cards were starting to mount up on my desk and I needed to do something. I set to work on finding a CRM (Customer Relationship Management) system that would support my growing networks. There are many cloud-based solutions on the market such as Salesforce.com and SugarCRM, it is worth researching to find a solution that meets your business needs. I now have full access to my 10,000+ contacts through my smart phone, at the touch of a button.

As it would be impossible for any one person to build a very strong and beneficial relationship with every single person, it can be helpful to work out who you really need to be spending time with. It is really about the quality of the contacts you have, and finding an effective strategy for communication.

Strong connections such as clients, referral partners, strategic alliances, close friends and family will clearly need more regular contact to maintain the relationship than a person you met two years ago at an event.

An effective way to categorise your contacts is to **P.I.N.G** them.

Priority - Contact every 1-2 weeks at least
Important - Contact every month at least
Normal - Contact every 2-3 months
Gone - Contact via Newsletter, or eliminate from database

Through the P.I.N.G system, you can easily stay in touch with the right people, which will lead you to more business. Having a CRM system makes it easy to target your marketing message at the people most likely to refer you.

You will be more successful, more quickly and create massive value from your network if you get this right. Once you are set up, keeping in regular contact across numerous touch-points is the key to effective relationship building. Devising a communication strategy for each type of contact will ensure that you can make the best use of your time and budget.

REFER AND CONNECT THE PEOPLE IN YOUR NETWORK

An effective way to ensure your network produces results, is to actively refer people you know, like and trust. Once you have confidence in their ability to deliver results, you can help them by giving them more business and they will want to do the same for you. As your network grows, you will continue to connect people and build relationships. Your network will become deep and wide across a range of industries and locations. In addition, you will find it easier to refer those around you.

My business is a manifestation of my personality, my core values, and myself; so, as a highly trained networker, it is important to me that my entire team 'buys in' to our way of working. We set referral and networking goals for the entire team – from Company Directors right through to the Administrative staff. Our goal is to give 500+ referrals per annum. In addition, we set targets against acts of giving, such as giving advice, providing testimonials for others, mentoring or showing gratitude. I call these our "giving goals."

As a business, we track our giving activity every week on an individual and team basis, so that we focus the entire company on giving, not getting. We know that this is the best way to generate results. Today, we are one of very few recruitment companies where no commission is paid to the recruitment team for placing candidates. This does not fit with the traditional model of the industry, which is typically all about sales, targets, commission and hunting. Our approach is based on farming relationships, account management and a total focus on customer service. Giving has become part of our culture, so referrals and connecting others has become natural to every team member.

Online networking can be very useful for making introductions for other people. LinkedIn allows you to make introductions, and give recommendations to others. At the time of writing this chapter, I have 2250+ connections on LinkedIn. This allows me to search and connect with over 12 million contacts within my network. This puts me in a strong position to refer or connect people. We are now one of the most connected small businesses in Ireland, and we refer and connect people on a daily basis. Thinking back to that day I relocated in 2005, I would never have thought that such a massive network would be possible. It gets much easier to grow our network, the more people who engage with our brand and our team.

KNOW YOUR TARGET MARKET

"You never know who people know." It's the old cliché. Back in the early days of starting my business, I was looking to be referred to multinational clients, but although I had been told that it was possible to get referred to larger companies, I was very sceptical about this. Meeting someone in Cork with the ability to refer me into a company like Google, Amazon, Facebook or Microsoft to me was unthinkable. How wrong could I be? A few months in, I decided to try it. I asked for a couple of large companies based in the Cork area, I named the company, location and the name of the person who I was looking to get a meeting with.

An Electrician, 30 years my senior, came up to me and gave me the name and contact details of the Head of the multinational company I had asked for, and they happened to be hiring. Up to this point, I had never dreamed that one of my best referrals would come from an Electrician. He had been wiring the new house of a Senior Director, Head of Ireland within an IT company. From that day, I knew the power of being specific and I have never again underestimated the contacts of people in my network. Joining BNI in 2005 trained me to be very specific about my target market.

The more people you can educate on who you are looking to talk to, the better. Always be prepared to provide names of your top five dream clients, you never know who people are connected to.

A way to find out the names of your target market is LinkedIn (www.linkedin.com). You can find out the name of any prospect, whether they are an IT Manager, Buyer, HR Manager, CEO or Financial Controller. Then educate your network to help you gain an introduction, by helping them understand the reason why the prospect would want to speak to you.

Answer the following questions for your business:

1. What value do you add to your clients and what makes you different from all of your competitors?
2. Who do you want to talk to – broad professions/categories?
3. Specifically who is on your top ten client list you would love to work with?
4. Your current client base. Show case studies of people you already work with.
5. What should they be listening out for that will trigger a referral?
6. What should they say or ask their contacts to make a referral happen?

Making it easy for your network to refer you is all about educating them on how to help you. Your contacts need to know this information and you need to know the same about them. That way you are in a strong position to give to, and to help, other people.

SAY THANK YOU

Thanking your network is a critical aspect of being an excellent networker. Today, one of our company goals is to send at least ten 'thank you' cards per week. Recognising people's efforts motivates them to want to help you more. In addition, the word-of-mouth about you and your company will spread. They will talk about you more, the card may even sit proudly in their office and you will be remembered. Because so few businesses do this, it helps us to stand out from our competition.

I still remember receiving a hand-written thank you card from someone who I had given a referral to. It had a positive quote on the inside and a customised picture specific to their business on the front. I was so touched that someone had taken the time to send this to me, it felt amazing to receive that card. Since then, I have integrated saying 'thank you' into my business across every employee.

But the thank you does not have to be a card. It can be a gift, a text message, an email or a letter. There are many creative ways to show you care. Recognition of people's efforts, and showing gratitude for what they do for us, has really helped the business to grow. More people remember and refer us because we always say thank-you.

Today, I train business owners around the world, inspiring them to achieve success through networking, word of mouth marketing, online reputation and referrals, all of which I am really passionate about. Anyone can do what I have done, all it takes is hard work, dedication and commitment. *Building The Ultimate Network* can get you to the point where over 90% of your new business is being referred to you. Set goals, learn more, and always be giving, then you can achieve anything you want from your very own ultimate network.

Chapter Author: Samantha Rathling (sam@expect-talent.com)

ABOUT SAMANTHA

Samantha Rathling is the Founder and Managing Director of Expect Talent, a unique recruitment business specialising in high-volume recruitment across all European languages. Samantha's vision and entire reason for being in business is to change the way the world does recruitment. Operating across the UK and Ireland, with plans to grow the business internationally, Samantha is a dynamic, driven and ambitious entrepreneur. She started the business at 28, and in less than 6 years has created a multi-million-turnover company.

Samantha is also Director of online business: ZeeSaw.com, which provides a platform for Companies across Europe to match and connect with commission only Sales Agents. This is a new venture for this serial entrepreneur and looks set to be another successful venture with the same passion and commitment to quality, service and results in a niche market.

Samantha is considered one of Ireland's best networkers, having built her businesses entirely through networking, word-of-mouth marketing, online reputation and referrals. As a BNI Director in Ireland South & West, and a key member of the BNI European Director Training team, she helps and supports members of BNI to grow their business through the power of "Givers Gain"®.

Samantha speaks internationally on the subject of networking, delivering engaging and captivating presentations to audiences across the world. Her story inspires and motivates people to engage with networking in a completely different way. She helps business owners to gain significant results by sharing hands-on experience, top tips and great methods, to build the ultimate network.

Learn more about Samantha at: www.samrathling.com
Visit her company websites: www.expect-talent.com & www.zeesaw.com

CHAPTER 21

OVERLOOKED NETWORK BUILDING OPPORTUNITIES

BY SHIRLEY PHEASANT

When considering the best opportunities to build your ultimate network, you will want to take a look at the multitude of openings happening in your own community. Many local not-for-profit organizations exist that are constantly short of volunteers with business expertise. You will quickly find you are welcomed into these communities where you will have the opportunity to work with other business professionals for the good of the community. It is a great way of giving back in a practical way for the business owner, plus it can be a fun way to build your ultimate network.

For example, many City Councils rely on not-for-profit organizations to run either a Main Street or similar Program. In this situation, there are several key areas where your business knowledge and enthusiasm for the local community can be put to good use.

PROMOTING YOUR COMMUNITY

Becoming involved in promoting your community will expose you to both consumers and business people, as you help to create marketing campaigns, retail promotions and special events. There is often a need for help with raising funds through sponsorships, giving you the chance to meet people from the top local businesses in a very different environment than that of trying to make your way through their gatekeeper.

DESIGN PLANS

Have a passion for historic buildings? Want to have a say in the look of your local community? This could be the perfect opportunity to combine your networking goals with your passions. Historic preservation is a hot topic for most communities, and showing your commitment in this area can bring you into contact with the most distinguished, senior local preservation advocates. These are, generally, people who have lived in the community for many years and they will "know" contacts that you could only dream about meeting.

ORGANIZATIONAL

No organization can exist without people working in the background who have business and organizational skills. The heart of the program will be its volunteers and that takes knowledge of recruitment and co-ordinating skills. You will find many of the volunteers are prominent local business people and your involvement will be noted.

ECONOMIC RESTRUCTURING

Whilst, at first glance, this may seem dreary in comparison to the bright lights of promotion or design, you ignore this area at your peril. You will gain direct access to business owners, both those already in the community and those who wish to re-locate into it. By focusing on the needs of the business community and supporting them with marketing information or techniques, you will find their willingness to refer you and your business grows exponentially. You may find yourself working closely with Development Departments in the City or County, and becoming that Go-To person for questions in the community.

BUSINESS OWNERS ASSOCIATIONS

In many Cities you will find there is a Business Owners Association, which is usually manned by volunteers, and they are always keen to bring you into the fold and introduce you around. You may be able to present a workshop, sponsor a breakfast or lunch, or just be one of the willing volunteers.

Something that will quickly become apparent to you, while investigating these opportunities and visiting the various groups, is that the committees are always looking for help with bringing structure and a business-like atmosphere to their meetings. Within the framework of the association you will have a wide range of participants from Retail, Trades, and Professionals, and many of the business owners are not skilled in preparing for meetings and they will benefit from working with someone, (you), if you are able to bring those skills to the group. If you have talents in simply being able to prepare a structured agenda and keeping meetings from dissolving into chaos, you will be home and dry!

The important part to remember is that you must first be prepared to give, before you can expect to receive. You will begin to establish your credibility with other business owners by being prepared to take on a leadership role, and showing your willingness to share your knowledge and expertise. This won't happen overnight; besides you will find there is much of interest to learn about how the community works, and you will want to find the niche that suits you and your skills and will display you in the best possible light.

WHERE TO LOOK

So, how do you find these hidden opportunities?

When you go to MAINSTREET.ORG you will find the National Trust Main Street Center website. From here you can search for a local Main Street Program in your State. Whilst at the site, be sure to check out the information surrounding the concept of the Main Street Program; this will give you more insight and get you started on thinking about where you will fit in. Contact the Program Director in your City or area, trust me, they will want to hear from you! Ask for a meeting with them, so that you can explore the possibilities available in more depth. These individuals are dedicated to the long term economic and historic health of their cities and you will be inspired by their knowledge and, in some cases, their fanaticism.

Type "Volunteer Opportunities in … (your local City/County)" into your search engine and you will find lots of sources for working with others for the good of your community. Be sure and go right to the top of the organization you are interested in, make contact with the President of the Board of Directors, or a Program Administrator, and meet with them to share ideas on how you can make a positive impact on the group.

Another great resource to explore is AmericanTowns.com. They are separated into States and then into Cities. Find your City and you will find links to local groups and organizations who need your help. Again, don't stop at a list of groups – pick a couple that sound interesting and meet with the organizers so that you have a good in-depth knowledge of what they do and how you can proceed.

WHICH TO CHOOSE

Once you have completed this research you will realize there are a multitude of opportunities for you to use your established skills, along with prospects for learning new ones. Now, you want to work out which of these opportunities will help you the most in building your ultimate network.

Obviously, if you have a particular passion for some of the organizations, this may be easy to identify. However, be prepared to diversify and take a good look at the people currently in the upper echelons of the group. If you are a Financial Planner, you probably don't want to be putting your hat in the ring of an organization that already has two or three Financial Planners who have been influential in the group for many years.

As a Commercial Real Estate Broker, (and, yes, I am truly passionate about commercial real estate!), I found the Economic Restructuring Team for our Main Street Organization was a natural fit.

I was not initially aware of the Main Street program in the City where I had purchased a Century 21 franchise, and was lucky enough to be introduced to the Executive Director through a referral partner in my BNI chapter, (The Leading Global Referral Marketing Network – check them out on BNI.com). As I mentioned before, some of these Main Street people are just plain inspirational! Here I was, fairly new to running my franchise, and thinking I might just be able to slide in to do a little volunteering, and I was faced with this whirlwind of enthusiasm and passion for *her* Main Street, Judy DeBella Thomas. She immediately alerted me to the opportunities that awaited me with Main Street, if I would only give her my first born! Oh no, that wasn't it, she only wanted my body and soul! Truthfully, I wanted to give it to her after that first meeting.

However, I am running a business, not a volunteer organization, so I considered what she had told me, thought carefully about where I could be the most help *and* where I thought I could get noticed. I joined the Economic Restructuring Team, (ERT), which met monthly, and began to contribute where I could. I'm not really someone who would normally push themselves into the forefront and make a big noise: I prefer to get noticed by providing effective information. There was another Commercial Real Estate Broker in the ERT when I began working with them, and he had been in the group for a while, but a funny thing happened – he started missing meetings, wasn't contributing anything positive to the program, and eventually he just dropped out. After about a year, I was asked to become the Chair for the ERT and I haven't looked back since. I have been really fortunate to meet, and work with, dedicated people who want to build our local community and help business owners grow and thrive.

Also, as a result of my involvement with Economic Restructuring, I was meeting monthly with the Business Owners Association and I have now chaired that group for two years. I have been able to help several of the business owners with one of my other passions, marketing, by sharing some workshops and they have shown their appreciation by passing me referrals to some great business opportunities.

TAKE ACTION TODAY

It can take a while to build long-term, strong relationships with business people you don't already have contact with, so begin today. Check out the websites and searches I mentioned above, (MAINSTREET.

ORG, "volunteer opportunities in (your town/city)", and AMERICAN-TOWNS.COM), this will give you a fast start in learning more about what is available in your area. Write down two or three categories that interest you immediately: it's a bit like playing Trivial Pursuit; your first answer is usually the right one. Now, importantly, call the top person you can reach in that organization, ask to meet with them as soon as possible, and let them know you are looking for a group that would benefit from your volunteer hours. That will probably be the easiest sales call of your life!

When you meet with the Program Administrator, or Executive Director, be sure to ask some searching questions. Is it a structured organization? What is their current focus? Are they part of a larger entity, (e.g. Main Street)? Do they have separate Committees or Teams within the group, and what are they? How can I be of the most help to your organization? What are the longer term plans for the group? Who else is part of the group and have they been supporters for a long time? What would be expected of me if I chose to join the volunteer group? You will naturally think of other important questions that may affect you directly.

Armed with this information, review your notes and make a choice. I would recommend you choose one organization and gauge how much time you actually spend in supporting them, rather than rushing into a commitment with several and then, perhaps, losing credibility if you can't follow up with your promises. Be careful not to spread yourself too thin: remember your goal is to build your ultimate network and you will want to be able to devote a reasonable amount of time to achieve this.

By taking a little time at the beginning of this project to do some research, you will find it will ease your learning curve as you meet with the various members of the organization, and make it much easier to decide on your particular niche within it.

ABOUT SHIRLEY

Shirley Pheasant is a native of London, England and became a Realtor in the United States in 2002. After finishing as Top Producer of her office in her first two years, she went on to pass her Broker exams in 2004. Her previous experience from the UK as an Information Technology Manager, with major emphasis on building and training a financial computer network, provided essential insights into the progress and growth of real estate on the Internet: a skill which has helped her embrace technology to push her business forward.

In May 2007 Shirley purchased a Century 21 franchise, Professional Realty in New Port Richey, Florida, and now runs a thriving real estate concern, which boasts specialists in Commercial, Investment, Residential and Property Management.

She is a dedicated member of the BNI Outlook To Success chapter in New Port Richey, Florida, has served as Vice-President on two occasions and now assists the BNI West Central Florida Director Team with Chapter Starts and Visitor Days. Shirley became a member of The Greater New Port Richey Main Street organization in 2008 and now serves on their Board of Directors, as Chair of the Economic Restructuring Team and Chair of the Business Owners Association. In her role as a Real Estate Broker and a member of the West Pasco Board of Realtors, Shirley also serves as Co-Chair for the Civic Affairs Committee.

Shirley is always glad to work with business people who want to be the best in their field, and willingly gives her time to find out how she can help them achieve their goals.

To speak with Shirley Pheasant, you can call her toll-free at 1-800 245 3303, or she will always answer your emails at: info@century21professional.com, and don't forget to visit the company website at: www.century21professional.com and sign up for her blog.

CHAPTER 22

COMMANDING THE ROOM

BY VICTORIA MAVIS, SPHR

Business professionals and others who want to build their ultimate network through connections from meetings, social events and other group activities can benefit greatly by learning how to successfully *Command the Room.*

Commanding the Room is the ability to easily connect with people through verbal and non-verbal communication in a manner that draws others into the conversation, thereby forming an instant relationship that leaves a long-lasting impression. It is that man or woman who exudes a level of charisma which others are attracted to and enjoy being around. It is much deeper than physical appearance.

Commanding the Room requires individuals to expand their networking skills to leverage time with each contact, conversation and relationship; thus, increasing the quality and depth of their network.

If you haven't had the personal experience of people being drawn to you, then you may want to dismiss this as a talent that can be learned. Before doing so, consider that anyone can be a 'personal magnet' if they take the time to learn, practice and perfect a few simple approaches.

CONFIDENCE

Commanding the Room requires a level of comfort in your own skin. Depending on circumstances, you may be filled with self-confidence or feel absolutely bankrupt of any ability to connect with people. To *Command the Room,* begin with assurance in who you are—which is partially based on past experiences and skills which you have developed over your lifetime; and also in the present—which are your thoughts or ideas at any given moment. To *Command the Room*, you first choose from where to draw your confidence.

Many years ago, I attended my first chamber mixer as a human resource consultant and quickly experienced failure through misguided confidence. I was an outsider walking into a room of business associates, equipped only with freshly printed business cards and confidence in the value of my professional knowledge.

Using Human Resources as my conversational launching pad, all self-assurance quickly eroded as everyone I spoke with dismissed any interest in what I knew. The final blow came when one business owner uttered the words, "I don't need any of that Personnel stuff" and walked away. Quickly retreating to a corner nearest the exit sign, I declared the event 'futile' for generating business contacts and prepared to leave. Then I met Don, and decided to stay and learn networking from a master at Commanding the Room.

Don worked as a property manager and was nearing retirement. His magnetism could be distinguished in any crowd by the style in which he engaged people in conversation. In meeting, his 6'4" frame towered over me as he placed a hand on my shoulder and said, "You're new, aren't you?" I squeaked, "Yes". With a big smile and a heart of southern charm he responded, "Let's go meet some other new folks."

Shadowing him that night, I learned the lessons of a lifetime by observing how easily he mingled with groups of known contacts as well as collections of strangers. Later, we withdrew from the crowd for a cup of coffee and a private conversation. When I asked what his secret was, he beamed, "I was put here for a purpose—and tonight that was to help others. When I do that, it'll come back ten-fold. When I don't, life just doesn't work as well."

As he finished speaking, I understood that a few of our paths had been very similar. Don experienced personal and professional success despite years of physical and medical issues that limited his mobility. His words cut to my core since I had a childhood accident which resulted a lifetime of walking limply. Although I sometimes felt that forearm crutches and my gait stuck out in the room like a purple Barney at a business meeting, his message reminded me that what really matters in life and business is how I treat people. With that as my foundation, it became easy to have a sure footing of self-confidence in every circumstance.

INTENTIONALITY

The next step in *Commanding the Room* is Intentionality. From the moment you first plan to attend an event until the minute it ends, your ability to successfully *Command the Room* is directly proportional to your level of preparation and commitment to a series of activities.

DO FIRST THINGS FIRST

Spend a little time researching hosted events. Who else is attending? Will there be any dignitaries, the press or other media? Request a schedule listing times for activities such as networking.

Occasionally, the basics get overlooked when attending an affair that does not model the typical networking event. Do you have business cards? Have you practiced your introduction? Do you have a pen? Notice, I didn't add, 'do you have flyers or a brochure?' *Commanding the Room* doesn't work when you try to sell people. Your only intent should be to engage with people you meet in a way that you are remembered by others, because of their positive experience.

READY, SET, ACTION!

Once at an event, your attitude can make the difference between it being another social outing or a huge success in your *Commanding the Room*. Walking into an area of strangers with the mindset of being at home, the first activity is to evaluate who is effective at engaging the biggest number of attendees in active conversation and therefore is *Commanding the Room*.

If you start searching for the person with the biggest title, the largest company, or the person who gets paid the most, you're headed in the wrong direction. Join the spheres where there is a storyteller with a diverse crowd and nestle up for some of their magic to sprinkle on you.

MAGICAL DUST

Once in a cluster of people whom you want to meet, your goal in *Commanding the Room* is for them to be left with something memorable on which you can establish trust and build a future relationship. This is done in conversation by comments, questions, or discussions that distinctly position you as someone in their network who provides a unique value.

To do this will often require a temporary shift in control of the conversation, especially when you join a group. This transfer must be done with elegance and transparency or else it appears as awkward as the mother-in-law upstaging the bride on her wedding day.

To be in command of a conversation long enough to make an ongoing impression begins with listening and when there is a lull in the dialogue, contributing a question or idea that is natural for the topic or audience. When responses indicate an interest in your direction, it shifts the focus of the discussion to you as the interim moderator. To be seen as adding value, requires that you balance the conversation between talking and listening. If you are the only one talking, it won't be long before the group sees you as another self-promoting salesperson.

Many networkers lack skills in sustaining conversations mainly because they are not good at asking questions that stimulate discussion. Every networker should have a set of questions memorized that are effective for engaging conversations. Whatever your list, I would add, "How do I know if someone I meet could benefit from your service?" The beauty in this question, as taught to me by my network, is that the response becomes a natural point for future action and follow-up.

After engaging in discussion where you have clearly differentiated yourself from others, what's next? Exit the group on a positive note by acknowledging the value of participant's questions, comments or ideas. It's appropriate to ask for business cards and permission for future contact. Lastly, ask if there's someone that you can introduce them to. If there is, make a point to deliver the introduction as soon as possible.

Thank all members and politely move to another group.

ONE SIZE FITS ONE SIZE

Considering the number of attendees at various events, it may be difficult for you to *Command the Room* based on sheer size. This is where advanced research will benefit you. *Commanding the Room* (or even a small corner) when there are 600 attendees requires a different tactic than when there are 50 participants. Chances are with bigger events you will know someone in attendance. The first step is to connect with a known contact and quickly form a networking tag team to help each other by sharing contacts through personal introductions.

This begins with identifying specifically who you want to be introduced to (name, position, company, industry) and your partner does the same. Next is to review with each other how you want the introduction to be delivered. Later, when introductions are made, monitor the conversation for a few moments to make sure the connection is complete, then excuse yourself and continue using this technique with other contacts in the room. If the introduction is stuck, nudge it a bit by bridging with a common interest between the two individuals.

HUMILITY

Sometime while *Commanding the Room*, you will most likely find yourself face-to-face with someone who has the ability to change the course of your life or your business, and you have their complete attention. Now what do you do or talk about? It is more important to understand what NOT to talk about.

Most people when in front of a potential prospect will unknowingly launch into self-promotion. According to Dr. Ivan Misner, "People go to networking events hoping to make sales contacts, but no one goes to these events hoping to be sold".

Your intent when introduced to a prospect is not to make a sales pitch or necessarily start a conversation. Rather, introduce what you do, make a lasting connection, be respectful of their time, and continue to network with other individuals. The key in all of this is how you spend the first two (and perhaps the only two) minutes with the prospect.

For me, I saw how this worked in reverse as I recall how I became a published author. Several years ago, I attended a conference and approached the host to thank him for the event. At the following year's conference, my team won recognition for top sales in our region and I once again met the host to thank him, but this time for the award we received. The third year, I noticed he had a workshop for authors and I was curious how I might be considered for a future team that he mentored. The fourth year, at the conclusion of his author workshop, I asked how I might be considered for the mentorship. He handed me his business card and indicated when and how I should email him. I did as he told me, along with the other program requirements and I was accepted into the next year's mentor program. Now, a year later, I am honored to be one of the co-authors of this book.

When I originally met the 'host', I approached him out of gratitude for what I gained by attending his organization's conference. Since that day, I use the opportunities when we meet to report on the usefulness of his conference in helping my network members grow their businesses.

GIVER'S GAIN

When I first began networking early in my professional life, I had the mindset "those with the most business cards at the end of the night, wins." Through years of networking, it has become apparent that it's not the size of my network that counts—rather it's the quality of contacts in my network that are committed to helping others that makes a difference.

Thanks to Don and others who have freely revealed their techniques, I can now easily *Command the Room* through the basics: Confidence, Intentionality, Humility and Giver's Gain.

You too, can benefit from what I've learned if you're willing to be coached by those more skilled than yourself, and if you go out of your comfort zone to embrace a new way to *Command the Room.*

ABOUT VICTORIA

Victoria Mavis, SPHR, also known as the *Queen of Coffee Conversations*^{TM} is a speaker, author and human resource (HR) expert that is regularly sought out by business owners and member organizations for her integrated approach in balancing people-programs with HR compliance to produce profits.

Victoria is known for always 'telling a story' to illustrate her experience from over 20 years in industries such as: hospitality, local government, manufacturing, medical services, non-profits, and retail. She skillfully guides clients to increased earnings by 'rightsizing' HR Administration including the use of human capital and Internet Technology.

Victoria speaks to audiences on HR Compliance Made Easy, Leveraging Employee Performance through Interpersonal Skills, and Achieving Professional Success Despite Personal Hurdles. As an individual who has had a physical disability since early childhood, Victoria inspires others to stretch beyond the limitations of their comfort zone in order to achieve a higher level of personal and professional success.

Victoria holds a MBA, is lifetime certified as a Senior Professional in Human Resources (SPHR) by the Society of Human Resource Management, and also certified as a Behavioral Specialist. She is a member of Rotary International, BNI, and other business, professional, and community organizations.

To learn more about Victoria Mavis, SPHR and how her HR programs can increase profits with limited resources while maintaining legal compliance, visit: www.hrknowledgebase.com or email her at: victoria@victoriamavis.com.

CHAPTER 23

TAKING YOUR NETWORKING TO A HIGHER LEVEL

BY RENA STRIEGEL

We all know someone who walks into the room and is instantly at ease. People gravitate toward them and meeting new people appears to be effortless. Yes, those social rock stars are out there. For the rest of you who do not get a standing ovation when you walk into the room, there is hope! In the same way that we can learn how to do complex math when we seem to have no natural ability for it, we can learn how to overcome and maximize our personalities to become effective, if not masters, at networking.

There are many aspects of personality that can cause us to trip up when a networking opportunity presents itself. The first thing that has to be acknowledged in order to become more effective at networking or any activity are your own weaknesses or hurdles, which prevent you from being successful. All personality types can experience challenges in a networking situation. It can be difficult to admit to anything that appears to put us at a disadvantage – especially in business. If you are introverted, walking into a large group, even if you know everyone in the room, can be extremely stressful. If you are extroverted, you may tend to socialize with friends and not make any new business connections. If you prefer that the spot light stay far away from you, approaching a complete stranger who is going to start asking you questions about you and your business can be pure agony. If you cannot think of what to ask someone after you discuss the weather and the score of last night's game, a two-hour networking event may make you feel as though a root canal is a more pleasurable way to spend your time. If you are walking into the event with the belief that no one will want to talk to you, you probably tend to avoid networking most of the time, because why would you go if you believe that no one wants to meet you?

CHECK YOUR MINDSET

Mindset is critical to successful networking. Many of my clients become paralyzed by the idea of going to a networking event. The key is to remember that a networking opportunity is just that – NETWORKING. It is a chance to make meaningful contacts that can help you in your business. If you believe that no one wants to meet you, your behavior will be drastically different than if you walk into a networking opportunity KNOWING that people WANT to meet you.

HAVE A GOAL

A goal? For networking? Yes! I encourage all of my clients to have a goal for their networking activities. The reason is simple: valuable resources (like time) are easy to waste when we aren't measuring the return on investment. If you talk to anyone, what is the number one complaint you are likely to hear? "I just don't have enough time." If time is one of your most valuable resources, why would you want to waste it by going to event after event with nothing to show for it? This holds true for those of you who find networking to be challenging, as well as for those of you who "love" to network. If networking is challenging for you, setting a goal can help you manage your anxiety in order to focus on the outcome that you are looking for. If you are extroverted, networking is often a "fun" release at the end of a stressful day, and you may find that you meet a lot of people but haven't gotten to know anyone.

Setting a goal can be as simple as deciding that you are going to meet two people that you would like to follow up with and get to know better after the event. Remember: networking should be an ongoing activity. You do not have to dominate the networking scene on the first try.

BE PREPARED

I know, most of you are thinking, "Duh!" This may seem like a no-brainer, but if you ever tried to compete in an athletic event without preparation, you experienced what participation without preparation feels like. It hurts. It is disappointing and it is more often than not a waste of time. The same holds true for networking. If you think about the times that you met someone and asked them for a business card, you can probably think of numerous times that they were unprepared and did not have a card. (Or, maybe you were the culprit that was not prepared!) Simple things like this can shape the impression that a new acquaintance is forming of you.

Being prepared can reach deeper than just having a business card on hand. The more you know about the networking event and who may be attending, the better prepared you will be to maximize the opportunity. Simple activities such as contacting the event coordinator prior to the event to introduce yourself and inquiring about who typically attends do two things: first, you have made your first connection and secondly, you know how many and what type of participants the event tends to attract. If you take advantage of the phone call, you can ask questions that will encourage the coordinator to think of introductions that she might be able to make for you. Now you know who you are looking for at the event. You have your "hit list", so to speak.

The better prepared we are, the less impact our own apprehension will have on the connections we can make.

FIND NETWORKING EVENTS THAT ATTRACT THE TYPE OF PROFESSIONALS/PEOPLE THAT YOU WANT TO MEET

There is no such thing as "one size fits all" networking events. Choosing events that fit your style and goals will dramatically increase the productivity of your network. Remember that networking events often are misnamed social events. If networking is your goal, you can quickly cross events where no networking is taking place off your list.

If you tend to freeze when faced with a large crowd of people, choose smaller more intimate events. If you appreciate structure (or need structure to maintain your focus), choose events that are more organized or have a portion of the event dedicated to introductions. If you meet people more easily in an event that is focused on fun rather than business, look for networking events that are organized around a sporting or other social event. If it takes you longer to warm up to people or you feel more comfortable in a setting that fosters long-term relationships, look for groups that meet regularly or require attendance.

TAG TEAM

If you want to maximize the number of professionals you can connect with at a networking opportunity, work the event with a "buddy". Once you have networked with several people together, split up. You will then be in the position of introducing your "buddy" as a "raving fan." If you have ever been introduced by someone who knows you well enough to rave about you, you know the power it has to break the ice, reinforce the introduction and move you quickly to a follow up meeting.

The Tag Team approach works well for everyone but is especially helpful if you have a hard time approaching new people, talking about yourself or connecting with people after the networking event. If you chose to employ this method, choose your "buddy" carefully. The key is to separate from each other so you can meet more people to introduce to each other. Beware of choosing a buddy that may cling to you or someone that you may end up hanging out in the corner talking to. Discuss your strategy prior to the event to ensure that you are on the same page and ready to go to work.

FIND THE SMILING FACE

Every event has one of them: The Smiling Face. The super-friendly person who greets and talks to everyone. Regardless of your networking abilities, The Smiling Face is a key connection at every networking event. The Smiling Face typically is a seasoned member of the networking group and knows most of the participants very well. The Smiling Face will be thrilled to meet you, excited to get to know you and will quickly introduce you to several of the attendees. If you want the quickest path to the core of the group, The Smiling Face is the ticket. If you are brave enough to admit to her that you are a bit nervous or intimidated to be in a room of new people, she will ensure that you are well-supported during the entire event.

For those of you who have no phobias of networking, try being The Smiling Face and watch what happens. You may find yourself making connections even easier than you already do!

GET INVOLVED

Once you have found the networking groups that resonate with you, taking a leadership position with that group should be your next task. Why? Early in my career, one of my mentors asked me, "Why would you want to sit in the room when you could be at the front of it?" This stuck with me and proved to be one of the best pieces of advice I ever received. Think about it. Who does everyone know? Who do people want to be close to? Who, because of their position, has the easiest time meeting visitors to the group? You got it – it is the leadership team.

Many of you are thinking I must be crazy! You are just getting up the courage to start attending networking events and now I am telling you that you should be in a leadership position. Take a deep breath. I am not telling you to be the President. Sitting on a committee is a great place to start. Then as you become more comfortable with the group, move up.

FOLLOW-UPS AND DOING WHAT YOU SAY YOU WILL DO

This is perhaps the biggest networking error of them all. How many times have you met someone, said you would connect with them and then never did? If you are not going to follow up, then what was the point of going to the event in the first place? The follow-up does not have to be in person (although this, in my opinion, is the best way to follow up.) You can follow up with an email, phone call or a note. The method is not as important as making the connection.

Meeting with people after the networking event is critical for two reasons: first, you solidify the introduction. Secondly, you determine what connection they are looking for so you can make it for them.

The quickest way to build a network of people that is working for you is to go to work for them. The most successful networkers are people who are willing to connect people and opportunities whenever they can. They become the "go-to" people. They are the people that are known for "knowing everyone." Why do you think that occurs? It is because they are consistently making connections for others. They have relationships with people that allow them to pick up the phone and create value for everyone involved. The best thing is it has very little to do with personality. It has everything to do with follow-through and willingness to be the connector.

Have you ever told someone that you would be in touch and then you forgot to follow up? Or, someone told you that they would introduce you to someone and they never did? How did you feel? Disappointed? Did you write them off as a resource? We tend to spend very little time developing relationships with people if one of these events has occurred.

BE OPEN, CONSISTENT AND DISCIPLINED!

Consistency is critical if you want your networking activities to pay off. You will not become the "go-to" person overnight. It takes discipline and a watchful eye to take advantage of every opportunity that you have to connect people. You can never have too many connections. The key is to make those connections more than just a name in your contacts directory. Again, this is an activity that may push you beyond the comfort zone that your personality would like to keep you in. You can employ the same techniques mentioned above to assist you in this. Plan and be prepared. You can research the connection before you meet with them. Check out their website and social media pages to create a list of questions, know what they are interested in, and get an idea of their background. You will be surprised more often than not that you have things in common, which can create a connection with that person very quickly and reduce the anxiety you may feel in meeting with them. Use the "buddy" system. Meet your new connection with your "buddy." Busy professionals always appreciate it when they can combine two meetings into one. Finally, find a way to bring value to the relationship. You want the connection to feel as though taking a meeting with you was a valuable use of their time.

YOUR PERSONALITY – PUT IT TO WORK FOR YOU!

Regardless of the challenges that you may face when networking, remember that your personality is what will attract your future connections. If you are not creating the network of professionals that you would like to have, take a few minutes to analyze your networking strategy and behavior to determine what is standing in the way of your success. You may need to enlist the help of a trusted friend who has been to events with you. Once you have determined how you can improve your technique or those behaviors you may need to correct, set your goals, chose an event that fits into your strategy, prepare to be successful, grab your buddy and go have some fun!

…. AND **DO NOT FORGET TO FOLLOW-UP!**

ABOUT RENA

Rena Striegel founded Empowered Business Strategies in 2006 after a 10-year career in the banking industry. After working with a wide variety of business owners in her role as Vice President of Private Banking, she began a full-time consulting practice focused on assisting business owners and executives implement best practices for greater business efficiency and profitability.

Rena has a passion for helping clients make more money and have more fun! She is known for being very hands-on in her approach to working with clients. By creating a strong working relationship with her clients, she is able to help them achieve the level of operational excellence that allows resources to be focused on growth rather than on fixing problems.

Rena is the president of the KC South chapter of Business Network International (BNI). Rena is a featured speaker at meetings and conferences throughout the Midwest on topics related to challenges that business owners face. In addition, she frequently offers free seminars and networking events structured to help business owners connect with strategic partners and resources.

Rena received her MBA from the University of Iowa in 2003, and her undergraduate degree in Sociology at Central College in Pella, Iowa. She is a certified coach and an adjunct professor at Mt. Mercy University and Webster University.

Rena lives in Olathe, Kansas with her furry office mates, Vela and Zara (Newfoundland dogs) as well as Tabitha and Gus (Persian cats).

CHAPTER 24

WHERE TO FIND YOUR ULTIMATE NETWORK

BY ALANA MCKINNEY

A ny woman will tell you that a hairdresser is worth her weight in gold if she can master the trifecta of style, cut and color. Lindy does that for me!

Several months ago after my appointment, Lindy whispered that she was leaving the salon that she had been with for 8 years and going "rogue". She had taken the plunge and signed a contract to open her own business about one mile from her current salon.

I made my next appointment, curious to see her new suite. The location was in the middle of new construction. Walking into the brand new building, there was a feel that one was entering an upscale resort spa.

Lindy's suite was equally as impressive. Along the right side there was a wall of colorful shampoos, creams, jells and foams. In the middle of the wall stood a large chair, huge mirror and deep black porcelain sink. In the corner was a beverage station with exotic teas and coffees as well as bottled water served in crystal wine glasses. Music played in the background that reflected the client's favorite genre. It was quite evident that much thought and consideration went into this business decision.

The left side of the suite was her office. A small table held her laptop, appointment cards, credit card terminal, as well as a very large appointment book that lay open.

We greeted each other warmly and I told her how impressed I was that she now was a full-fledged entrepreneur. I could see, however, that she was a little hesitant about something.

"Alana, I love being a hairdresser and I am good at it, but there is more to running your own business than being good at what you do. I thought clients would bring me all the referrals I would ever need. That's not happening."

Our conversation led me to ask "What is your marketing strategy for your first year in business, Lindy?" She explained her plan was to put an ad in the local paper and the yellow pages. Also, keeping in touch with her previous clients through mailings and phone calls was a top priority.

A delusion that many entrepreneurs have when starting a business is that potential clients will be referred to them from their current customer base because of their great products and exceptional service.

Looking at successful business owners who have many clients walking through their door may cause an entrepreneur to be jealous, and wonder if they ever would get to that point. In reality, it is not hard. The trick is to know where to look for your target networks, and what to say and do when you find them, that will guarantee you having a growing, thriving business.

I asked if she was open for some advice. Lindy gave me an enthusiastic "Yes." I proceeded to share with her where five networks were that could potentially supply her with referrals, endless clients, business coaches, and a marketing advisory board. The cost would be affordable if she was willing to be pro-active and not wait for the referrals to fall into her lap.

1. LOOK FOR AN INCLUSIVE NETWORK

First, find and participate in an open or inclusive network group. A local Chamber of Commerce, Rotary, or Lions Club meeting once or twice a month would be such a group. An important concept to remember is that you are going to introduce yourself, your products, services and the geographical location of where you do business. This is not a time to sell. Think back to when you registered to attend a Chamber meeting, did you think, "I can't wait to go shopping at my business meeting." It would be rare to see that scenario. Don't expect the other attendees to be going to shop either. Events of this type are designed to let the business community know that you are in business. Your credibility will increase substantially if you volunteer within the group. A good way to think about this is picture yourself as a host no matter how new you are to the organization. Many members will relax around you if you are seen as a giver of your time and talents and not there just to sell. An open network group also means that your competition more than likely will be attending events shoulder-to-shoulder with you. Stay focused on why you joined and you can move this to your advantage.

Lindy joined her local Chamber of Commerce and volunteered to be a greeter host. She stationed herself at the entrance and introduced herself to the business community as they came into the room for the monthly events. I encouraged her to read Masters of Networking by Ivan R Misner PhD. and Don Morgan M.A., and especially highlighted the chapter "The Networker's Best Ammunition" by Bob Berg, contributing author. In his chapter, Bob gives 10 Networking Questions That Work Every Time. Greeting and starting a conversation in a fun and friendly manner will go a long way to build rapport when it does come time to sell. I assured her that using these "nuggets of advice" would put her head and shoulders above the competition.

2. LOOK FOR A EXCLUSIVE NETWORK

Second, join one closed or exclusive networking group. A definition of an exclusive network group is a group that meets regularly (usually once a week), there is one business professional per category as a member in the group, and the purpose is to give tips, leads or referrals. Examples of closed networking groups are Le Tip, Leads Club and Business Network International (BNI). There is a higher caliber of business that is done within an exclusive group of business professionals because relationships are "queen." It takes time to build a culture that has trust. If you give the time and energy involved to create or be a part of an exclusive group, then it will not be easily broken or disbanded. The social capital in a closed contact group can bring you wealth far above monetary gain. In the first year of membership, many members experience camaraderie that leads to a high level of trust, referrals that expect your call, and more value and money generated per client. The second year and beyond, members who build on the foundations of their first year of membership can experience self-improvement, better communication skills, and develop into a more savvy, educated consumer. If you are a person who works extensively with online social media to generate business, this type of group could be a shock to your system. It is still common knowledge among professionals in the word-of-mouth networking industry, that the best way to build and accelerate trust that leads to a more profitable business, is to meet weekly in a structured environment. Lindy knew that finding the right closed-contact group was important, and she wanted to interview several groups before committing to one group over the other.

With her iPad in hand she developed questions to ask each group when visiting. How long has your group been in existence? How many members do you have? Do you meet weekly? Is there a system you follow so all the members know what is expected of them? Are there trainings and mentors to help a new businessperson build a strong business? What is the monetary amount of the closed business from referrals that your group has generated to date? With questions in hand, Lindy went to visit an actual meeting and meet the folks. She knew she needed to attend a meeting to determine the energy and personality of the exclusive group.

3. LOOK FOR YOUR INDUSTRY'S CONFERENCES, SEMINARS, WORKSHOPS

Third, be sure that you attend the conferences, seminars, workshops held in your industry. Obtain a roster of attendees before the event and search for the top-producing professionals in your field that will be attending. Schedule a one-to-one interview during your conference that should take no longer than one hour. Be sure that you stick to the time agreed upon. If it looks like you will be going over, ask for additional time. Most high achieving business professionals are happy to have a mentoring session with someone who is willing to listen, take notes and consider implementing the wisdom that is shared. Before the conference and interview, send a little personal information on yourself.

Consider providing some of your personal and business goals, achievements, interests, networks you have joined and some of your skills. Let your 'interviewee' know that you would be interested in learning more about them, as well as "What is working for you in our industry and what is not?"

Lindy had one large seminar that she attended each year. There was no question who she wanted to interview. Year after year, this person was recognized at the Recognition Gala with top honors in most new clients gained in the previous year. I told her if she ever wanted to interview this person again or someone of their caliber in the future, remember you have two ears and one mouth and the good Lord expects you to use them proportionally!

4. LOOK FOR STRATEGIC ALLIANCE PARTNERS

Fourth, build a group of diverse businesses that you can call on if your clients should need a trusted referral. Let the businesses know that you would like to refer them to your clients, and in return, you would like them to do the same for their clients when their clients should need your goods or services. A group of two or more businesses that make a commitment to pass referrals to a common target market is called a Strategic Alliance Partnership. Strategic Alliance Partners are not in competition, but complement each other. When building this specialized network, ask the question, "Would I use this business for my own family, friends or very best client?" Keep in mind, when you give a referral, you are giving your credibility as well. As a rule of thumb, people will "share" more about the referral that "bombed," than the referral that went well.

A target market that Lindy enjoys working with are brides and their attendants. Several Strategic Alliance Partners that could bring value to Lindy's services could be: Mary Kay Consultant, nail tech, costume jewelry provider, fine jewelry Jeweler, florist, event planner, travel agent, caterer, men's clothier, Send-Out-Cards Representive, real estate agent, cleaning service, rent-all business, and a mortgage professional.

5. LOOK TO BECOME A CONNECTOR BETWEEN YOUR CLIENTS AND YOUR NETWORKS

Once a business has found their *Ultimate* Network, it does take some maintenance and PR to keep it functioning smoothly. Be sure that you keep in regular touch with the businesses that you have built a relationship with. Keep them in the loop of who you would like to be introduced to, or what project or contest has special needs that they can provide. Remember this is a two-way street. Always approach your business relationships as, how may I help you before you help me?

Let your clients know you have worked to develop a Team of business professionals and trades folks willing to help fill the needs of your valued clients.

Lindy created an online newsletter and featured one of her partnerships each month. There was a theme throughout the letter that helped Lindy to maximize her referral partnership. She did not give the contact info in the newsletter because she wanted her clients to contact her even if they did not need her goods or services at the time. She changed her email signature to read a new referral partner each month. "If you find yourself in need of a licensed home inspector please contact me either by email or phone. I will be happy to introduce you. She knew if she branded herself as the "go-to gal" for all of her client's needs, her customers would definitely call her when they needed a style, cut or color.

ABOUT ALANA

Alana McKinney is the Entrepreneur's Networking Advocate by taking the mystery out of Social Capital.

She discovered the power of networking years ago, when a gun shop opened across from her children's high school. Realizing she couldn't change the situation on her own, Alana reached out to others—including First Lady Hillary Clinton, the late Senator Henry Hyde, and Sarah and Jim Brady. Her crusade was picked up nationally, and the gun shop agreed to move.

Alana then used networking to expand her women's clothing business. This brought her into contact with Business Network International (BNI). Its philosophy of "Givers Gain" spoke to her. Alana became an Executive Director and Partner for the Chicago-land region, responsible for the operations, marketing/PR and nurturing of a franchise of more than 80 BNI chapters.

Today, Alana advocates the benefits of networking and word-of-mouth referral marketing to BNI members, entrepreneurs, businesspeople and not-for-profits. She is a frequent presenter and coach on networking strategies and techniques. Alana has worked with Action Coach International, The Brian Buffini Organization, Herbal Life, Mary Kay Cosmetics, SendOutCards, Shaklee Corporation, and Signs By Tomorrow, among many others.

Alana has been featured on The Oprah Winfrey Show, The Today Show, NBC Nightly News, CNN, ABC, NBC and CBS, as well as in *The Chicago Tribune*, *The Chicago Sun-Times*, and on radio interviews.

Her favorite saying is:– *Intelligent people know facts; successful people know people.*

To learn more about Alana, to arrange a networking speaking engagement or coaching relationship, contact her at: Contact@AlanaMcKinney.com, or visit her blog at: www.AlanaMcKinney.com.

CHAPTER 25

MAKE A GOOD IMPRESSION THAT LASTS

BY MARJORIE S. COWAN

arly in my professional life I learned the value of making a good impression that lasts, and having a well-planned thirty to sixty-second presentation. I was at a convention when a distinguished lady walked up to me and asked, "What do you do?" As I stammered and stuttered, trying to think about and formulate what to say, I could see in her eyes that I was losing her interest and her desire to talk with me. Have you ever had this experience? Someone asks you what you do, and while you are trying to formulate the correct answer, you fail to make a good first impression. You may even begin to articulate what it is you do, and get a polite response, but you know that you have lost their attention and interest. The result is that you wind up feeling un-professional, and have the awareness that you might have just missed out on an important connection.

There is a very good explanation for this all too familiar phenomenon, as you will discover when you read below. In addition, to keep from having this experience, you must give thought and preparation time to what it is about you that fails to make a good impression on others. And then you must prepare and rehearse the calm, confident, and competent short presentation designed for that situation. And, yes, this does mean you need to have several presentations prepared.

WHAT TYPE ARE YOU?

Over the years I have noticed that there are many ways people respond to the question, "What do you do?" The first four types that are most prominent are the "Anxious Responder," the "Indifferent Responder," the "Obnoxious Responder" and the "Overconfident Responder." All four types fail to make a good first impression on other people. The final type is the "Competent Responder" who usually makes a good and lasting impression.

THE ANXIOUS RESPONDER

Researchers tell us that many people fear public speaking more than they fear death. Imagine that. I call this type of person the "Anxious Responder." For this type of person, death would be a welcomed alternative to having to speak in public, or even to a stranger for that matter. This type of person is so caught up in the notion of what other people are thinking of them that they become immobilized. They have little room for an adequate presentation. They fear the judgment of others or shame of being inadequate so much, that they think what they say has to be perfect.

For example, I know an accountant, Sally, who planned a sixty-second presentation about her accounting business and then used the same talk with absolutely everyone she met. She never customized her talk for an individual or for different groups. She had an extensive list of every service her company offered and she read it out to everyone and did not share any benefits of her services. At her BNI meeting, the world's most successful business referral organization, she gave the same presentation every week. She even held up a tattered 3x5 index card every week with her talk on it. The members knew what to expect and, therefore, did not listen. She wondered why she was not receiving very many referrals. Once she gained the insight and confidence to add new material, to give some specific details and benefits about one of her services, and to be able to think on her feet, referrals started coming in to her.

As a Dale Carnegie Course Instructor for many years, I realized that many people are more concerned about what others are thinking about them than what they are trying to communicate about themselves. In their attempt to be perfect, correct, and acceptable, they feel overwhelmed and inadequate and lose their listeners.

THE INDIFFERENT RESPONDER

Of course there are some people who just don't see or feel the need to make any preparation toward making a lasting impression. I call this person the "Indifferent Responder," because they really don't care what others think about them.

Years ago I was the member of a BNI referral group that had a nice fellow as a handyman. However, each time he stood to make his sixty-second presentation, he said, "Hi, I'm Joe your friendly Handyman. You all know what I do. Send me some business." This took about eight seconds and then he would sit down. Joe obviously gave little thought to the real purpose of his sixty-second presentation, which was to educate his referral sources. He missed the opportunity to educate his colleagues about the scope of his skills. He missed out on guiding their imagination about the kind of problems he could repair and the type of people who could use his services. Joe was a nice guy, and he was a skilled handyman, but it wasn't long before his group stopped making referrals to him.

The interesting thing about people similar to Joe the Handyman is that they don't have enough anxiety and good old-fashioned drive to put forth the energy to prepare for the presentation. It is no big deal to them if people are attracted to them or not. People like Joe never worry about things like success and advancement in their respective businesses.

THE OBNOXIOUS RESPONDER

There is another group of people who are just plain "Obnoxious Responders." They make a lasting impression on you; just not the kind of good encounter you look forward to experiencing again. Recently a colleague told me of an incident that happened to him at a networking meeting visitor's day. A woman said to him, "I will join your group if you will become my client." He demurred by saying, "That's not how it works. You would need to join the BNI Chapter on its own merits."

To which the woman replied, "Well, you look six months pregnant and your skin is grey and sickly, and you need my help." His response was to tell her that she didn't know him or anything about him. To which she replied that she had been trained to see illness in people and he obviously needed her help. In addition, she told him if he was already working with a personal trainer, it was certainly not helping him.

It is truly amazing that some people believe they can insult people into being their clients. They experience other people as objects in their world rather than living feeling people.

THE OVERCONFIDENT RESPONDER

The final type of ineffective people is the "Overconfident Responder." This type really believes that everything they say is so enthralling that everyone will want to listen to them with admiration and awe. They rarely plan out what they are going to say which is apparent because they tend to ramble and believe their charisma will impress everyone within listening distance. They also tend to monopolize any conversation and, if there are time limits imposed for a presentation, they ignore them and can become indignant if they are enforced. They truly love the sound of their own voice.

I know a Business Coach, Ken, who was the epitome of an Overconfident Responder. It was apparent he was planning what he was going to say as he was standing up and he always talked on and on. It was true that Ken had a lot of charm and a great smile. It was also true that when he was in an informal group situation he never focused on the person with whom he was talking. He was always looking around to see who else he should impress with his presence.

Of these four types of people, the Obnoxious Responder, the Indifferent Responder and the Overconfident Responder see no need to grow and change. The Indifferent Responder has no urgency to change or grow, the Obnoxious Responder lives with the self-assured arrogance that only he or she is right, and the Overconfident Responder truly believes that he or she is gifted. All are convinced that any problems or rejection they may experience in life are caused by other people.

Ironically, it is the Anxious Responder that can make the most change and growth toward becoming a Competent Responder and accomplish the goal of making a good, lasting impression. The truth is, most of us, at one time or another, have fallen into the Anxious Responder Category. Why is this type of person capable of the most change? Because the Anxious Responder still respects and values other people and their opinions. This type of person also has a sense of wanting to be recognized and respected for who they are. They just need coaching, guidance and practice on how to get there.

Now that we know the problems with making a good first impression, we can move on to how to create the change that brings about the calm and confident Competent Responder.

PRACTICE YOUR ROLE

Nothing takes the place of practice and rehearsing the part of the calm, confident, and competent person. You might be surprised that quite a few actors suffer from stage fright. Some even take a Beta Blocker medication, prescribed by a psychiatrist, before they go on stage. Why should we be surprised when stage fright happens to us?

My most memorable experience of an Anxious Responder, with acute stage fright, that became a Competent Responder was with a class member I had in a Dale Carnegie Course. This person was so incapacitated by fear that every morning he would have breakfast in the diner where his wife worked, and would sit in a back booth and hold a newspaper in front of his face so he would not have to talk to or see people. During the class, he challenged himself to move from the hidden back booth to a chair at the counter and put the newspaper down. He was stunned to find out that people actually wanted to talk with him and thought he was an interesting person. By the end of the class, he was pouring coffee for the patrons at the diner.

Through the Dale Carnegie Course he was exposed to a safe training environment where he could rehearse the part and was given positive feedback on his progress. BNI offers another safe location to rehearse and practice presentations. Meeting with a group of business colleagues each week helps a person develop the trust needed to confidently give thirty to sixty-second presentations. The Toastmasters organization is yet another type of experience that offers a person a chance to be spontaneous and rehearse presenting.

REMEMBER, SECONDS COUNT

When you start making presentations you will learn very quickly that seconds count. There are a lot of factors that make up the human attention span, but psychologists tell us that a person's focused attention, which may be from 5 to 15 seconds, is the short-term response to a stimulus that attracts attention. In other words, it is that very brief window of opportunity to which you must focus your personality and personal presentation in order to capture another person's interest.

Have you ever listened to a two-minute radio commercial? I suspect you haven't. Why? Because the industry understands that the most effective commercials are under one minute, and they must capture the listener's attention in the first few seconds or lose the listener. The TV Industry has longer commercials, but they have the added benefit of a lot of visual stimulation. Even so, lately I have sat back after watching a commercial on TV and said to myself, "What was that about?" I didn't even remember the product that was being advertised.

Seconds do count! Therefore, you must prepare your presentations for any encounter by having an attention magnet that captures a person's interest and imagination before another distraction, such as an internal thought, piece of jewelry, a flash of light, or another person's smile comes into their field of view.

I was at a BNI networking meeting a few months ago listening to several business professionals talk about their companies. What struck me is that some of them immediately commanded my attention and interest and others gave me time to take a mental vacation. What made the difference? The ones I remembered had an attention grabbing statement. The human brain processes information so fast that while someone may be present in a meeting and appear to be listening, they can be far away working on a problem or day-dreaming. Our job is to pull them back to the here and now and have them want to listen to us. Ways to accomplish the attention are by: Making a shocking or a thought-provoking statement, asking a question, changing pitch or volume without yelling or being strident, or having a prop or demonstration are ways to keep them listening.

PLANNING THE PRESENTATION

To plan and prepare for a short presentation, first go into your analytical mode. What is your goal? Step back and analyze your location and audience. What is appropriate? Do you want them to remember you? Do you want to educate them about your products or services? Do you want to motivate them to use your business? Do you want to motivate them to refer others to you? Plan what you want to say with the desired outcome in mind.

Members of BNI have the opportunity to give a sixty-second presentation every week. The setting and audience lends itself to educational and motivational presentations. The goal is to educate the other members about the product or service and to motivate them to find referrals during the week. Even in this structured environment where there is a captive audience, it is still necessary to capture the attention and interest of everyone there.

Preparing and practicing short presentations for the person we meet in the elevator or at a Chamber of Commerce Business After Hours is crucial. Short, powerful and colorful statements about who we are and what we do professionally can capture the attention and interest of the listener. The goal is to have them ask us questions. When they do, we can expand on our product or service and the benefits. To someone with red eyes and a tissue in the spring, a heating professional might say, "I help people breathe deep healthy fresh air in their homes and offices and avoid the watery eyes, sneezing fits and hacking cough," rather than "I sell heating and air conditioning."

What is it you want the person to remember? Not just your product or service, but you, your sincerity, your credibility, and your trustworthiness. Don't get caught up in the process of selling your products or services to the point that you forget that you are really selling yourself. Although I don't even remember the magazine, one of my favorite magazine covers was from years ago. On it were two actors, one dressed as a priest with a clerical collar and the other was a prostitute. The title was, "Everyone is in sales. The only difference is what you are selling!" How profound! We forget that we are all "selling" every day, all day.

THE BEST WAY FOR PEOPLE TO REMEMBER IS WITH STORIES AND NOT JUST FACTS.

People remember stories and not facts. You probably have stories of satisfied customers using your products or services and benefiting from them. Tell the stories while protecting the identity of your clients. If the stories are action packed, inspirational or motivating, that is even better. When telling the stories, relive the experience so they are heartfelt and genuine. Create a collection of stories to which you can refer at any time.

SUMMARY

If you are having trouble making good, lasting first impressions, here are four action steps you can initiate today to help you become a good lasting impression in someone's mind:

1. **Ask yourself, "What type am I?"** If you are like the Anxious Responder, and so many of us are, take heart. There is hope that with some positive reinforcement, you will find that most people are just like you. Most of us are afraid of being judged or criticized. The goal is to become a Competent Responder, where people look forward to listening to and communicating with you.

2. **Develop four or five short presentations.** Plan and rehearse with a trusted friend who will give you honest feedback, three or four 30 to 60-second presentations that describe how you and your business are unique and focus on the benefits. Put your own personality into the presentations and tell stories.

3. **Develop a practice arena.** Joining a BNI referral organization chapter and a Toastmasters Club and take a Dale Carnegie Course to give you ample exposure and practice time where you can grow calm, confident and competent in presenting yourself and what you do.

4. **Practice, Practice, Practice!** Practice probably doesn't make perfect, but it gets you close. Besides, perfection is not the goal. Sincerity, honesty, integrity, and competency are the goals. Become confident in presenting the benefits of your product or service and telling stories. It is good to have a few butterflies in your stomach before a presentation and it is best when the butterflies fly in formation.

ABOUT MARJORIE

Dr. Margie Cowan, an Executive Director, owner and CEO of BNI of Colorado and Southeast Wyoming, is a New York Times bestselling author and educator. She is an expert in business networking and has been sought out internationally as a speaker. She is the BNI USA Senior Training Director. She has served BNI International on its Founder Circle.

Margie is a sales and communication skills trainer and speaker, entrepreneur and real estate broker. She was an instructor for the Dale Carnegie Courses, and the National Association of Realtors, Certified Real Estate Brokerage courses. She was honored to have been the Realtor-Associate of the Year for the State of Georgia.

With her husband Emory, Margie makes her home in Colorado where they enjoy the mountain grandeur and visits from their grandchildren. They also live part-time in the Los Angeles, California area.

CHAPTER 26

BUILDING THE ULTIMATE PRODUCT PROMOTION NETWORK

BY GREG ROLLETT

Y ou have been working hard over the past few weeks, or even months creating your new product or service. You have all the ins and out, features and benefits and all the technology (or offline storefronts) tested to give your new customers an enjoyable user experience.

The only problem is...

you have no customers. No one is walking by your store, or coming to your website. And it's such a shame since you have such an amazing product.

For those starting out you may do some traditional advertising, on tv, radio or the newspaper. Maybe even jump into a Groupon or Living Social and create a deal of the day. For online marketers, you are probably thinking about pay-per-click, or SEO, social media or one of those fancy "free traffic magic button" courses that are all over the Internet.

And yes, while these advertising methods will bring you a possible infusion of customers, I want to help you create a powerful network to help not only to build your business, but to grow with your business.

You see, there are already a great deal of people that have customer and prospect lists for the exact people that would greatly benefit from your product or service. They have done their own hard work to market to and collect information over the course of their own business's lifespan.

I want you to be able to take advantage of that data while in turn helping them grow their business and providing value to their audience. I call this strategy Leveraging Other People's Audience and as you read this chapter I encourage you to take notes and realize the potential in your own business to sell your own products and services.

THE 4 STEPS TO BUILDING YOUR ULTIMATE PRODUCT PROMOTION NETWORK

STEP 1: MARKET RESEARCH

If you have just completed creating an exceptional product you should have done some initial testing and market research to see:

- Who your ideal customer is
- What their problem is
- What solution they are looking for
- Who is currently offering them that solution
- What makes your solution better, more unique, different, faster, stronger, etc

We need to revisit these core principles in the first step of building our network. In order to find other small business owners and businesses with similar interests we need to dig down and define who our customer is.

If we do not know this data, it makes it difficult to start asking people to send out our product information to their own closely guarded customers.

The best way to tell if you really know your ideal customers is to do a quick test. For this test you will need a piece of paper. Once you have this piece of paper, fold it in half length wise.

On the left side of the paper write down the name of your favorite character in the Simpsons. You can choose Homer, Bart, Marge, Lisa, Apu,

Mr. Burns, even Smithers.

Then I want you to write down everything you know about them including:

The clothes they wear
Their hairstyle
What they do for a living
Who their friends are
What they spend their money on
How they enjoy spending their time
And any other details about them that you feel add to their character.

If you chose Bart Simpson, you might have written down that he wears an orange shirt with blue shorts, has spikey hair, goes to Springfield Elementary where he hangs out with Milhouse, spending his money on comic books and slurpees, spending time in his backyard tree house and constantly causing trouble in the neighborhood.

Not a bad description, right?

Now, on the right side of your paper is your true moment of truth. Write down the name of your ideal customer. Then go down and answer the same questions about them, especially how they are spending their money, what they do for a living and who their friends are.

I hope you see where I am going with this. If you were able to complete this exercise you are ready to move onto part 2 in creating your product promotion network. If not, you really need to look at who your business serves and what problem you solve in the marketplace.

PART 2: FINDING YOUR NEW PRODUCT PROMOTING NETWORK

Once you know who your ideal customer is, you can start looking for businesses that are already marketing to, and have a customer list full of them.

The first place I like to look is online. Through social networks, online directories and the powers of search engines there is an unlimited amount of power right in open, ready for you to cultivate and help your business grow.

There are a few powerful tools that we are going to use to funnel all this information and give us actionable content that we can use to build our network. The first is a nice spreadsheet.

Without this spreadsheet, the rest of this section is going to be very difficult to manage. On this spreadsheet you are going to want to create columns for:

- Site name
- URL
- Email address
- Phone number
- Skype ID
- Facebook page
- Twitter handle
- YouTube profile
- And a notes section

Each section should be pretty straightforward as to what information goes into each column as you fill it out. For those of that are extremely busy, the following information can easily be handed to a virtual assistant, office manager or even an intern to complete so that you can go ahead and start building the real relationships with this list.

Now that we are prepared we can start on a site called AllTop.com. At AllTop.com you will find a list of all the top websites broken down by category. So if you were in the legal niche, you might look for categories such as Law, Legal, Patents, Copyright, Family Law, US Senate and other categories of interest.

Once you land on this category you will be shown all the top websites, blogs, news sites and more that pertain to that category. I want you now to click on each link, look at every site and see if it would be a good fit for your products or services, if you enjoy the content, if they have active readers leaving comments or participating and sharing within social media and even looking at the traffic for the site (using tools like Compete.com or Alexa.com).

If you feel it is a fit, go ahead and put it into the spreadsheet. If not, no worries, move onto the next one.

Once you go through AllTop.com you will want to move into social media and find the power users on each platform. I would start with Facebook. In the top search bar, again search for your main keywords. When you do so you will have the ability to filter by group, page, events and more.

You want to find the groups and pages with the largest number of active participants. Go ahead and join the groups and like the pages. Befriend the administrators. And then again go ahead and fill in the spreadsheet with the information you have found.

After you conquer Facebook I want you to turn your attention to You-Tube. Again perform a few searches for your top keywords that address your market. On YouTube you want to use keywords that are more geared towards actions, or videos that help solve your customers problems. To find these a simple tactic is to insert "how to" at the start of your search query, so an example may be "how to perform a basic yoga pose" or "how to protect my assets for my children."

You are looking for videos with high view counts, positive user comments and feedback and any other characteristics tha might compliment your own business. Again, make note of their profile URL's and all of the other information needed for the spreadsheet.

The last place we are going to venture today is Twitter. With Twitter there are 2 great directories for us to use to collect power user data. They are Twellow and WeFollow. On both of these sites you will find a directory of Twitter users again broken down by category. Find the ones that are of interest to you and sort them by number of followers.

When on their profiles again you are looking for engagement, check out the links back to their sites, what they Tweet about and who their audience is. If they are a good fit add them to the spreadsheet.

After going through the resources above, there is no reason that you shouldn't have a list of 50-100 authority figures in your niche that will be the start of your product promotion network.

STEP 3: MAKE CONTACT AND ADD VALUE

You didn't think we made that list just to feel good about looking at it right? Good. The third step in our plan to grow our business for the long term is to start cultivating relationships with all the people on that list.

When getting started there are some basic tactics that you can do to show interest in the market and start getting them to notice who you are.

The first of which is promoting them in your own social sphere. You can do this by leveraging your own Twitter and Facebook accounts and share their latest links, blog posts and articles to your followers. When you do this be sure to tag them, mention them or use their name so they are notified that you did mention them.

At this stage you are expecting nothing in return, but you are creating good will and showing that you respect the content that they are creating and wanted to share it with your won crowd.

For those that like to stay organized, I recommend creating a few more columns in that spreadsheet to indicate which people we have mentioned through social media and on what dates. Again this portion can be done either by yourself or an assistant.

The next step is to lightly engage them. This can be done by commenting on a blog post, sending them a direct reply on Twitter or even messaging them or sending a friend request on Facebook. This step is best approached after you have caught their attention in the social world as it will bring a familiarity with you and make the invite more appealing than someone who just stepped in off the curb.

And now it's time to strike. Once they know who you are, most people are going to check you out right back. I always want to know who the person is that just commented on my site, asked me a great question on Twitter and shot me a quick message or tip on Facebook. That's human nature and intrigue right there.

If you have a great brand and foundation for your business, when they check you out they will see the like interests and that you are working in the same field. Now the approach becomes even greater in your favor as you look like the fresh face in the industry.

Once you have their attention it is time to wow them with value. Remember in the research phase I asked you what made your product different, better, stronger or faster? This is where it comes into play.

You need to find the missing link that compliments what they are offering to the market. If you are both yoga instructors, how do your teachings differ? Do they focus on weight loss and you focus on posture? Do you have a certain framework that will help their audience get results faster so they can graduate into this person's intermediate classes?\

Once you find that missing piece and you can do it with 5-10 big players in your market, you have now created an incredible team that all works together to serve similar markets without having to create products and services for all the variables in the market.

When I first started in the music marketing niche, I needed to find my differentiating factor. While some other big players were talking about record deals, or how to get music in tv and film, I focused on email marketing and building a fan base. This complimented the record label guy as having a fan base is attractive to getting a record deal.

We were able to provide value to each other and grow both of our businesses and sell more of our products which brings us to...

STEP 4: UTILIZING YOUR NEW PRODUCT PROMOTION NETWORK

You have now successfully built an entire network of influential players in your market and are providing them extreme value, while they compliment your own products and services.

Now is the time to create your outline for the year and plug them all into your system. You see, if everyone is heavily promoting at the same time, no one wins. The customers get beat up and sales go down. But if you strategically plan out your product launches, promotions and events evenly throughout the year, you will all win.

Let me explain. You see, at this point you are still possibly only thinking about your product. And while you are going to be selling more and more of your product, you now also have an entire market of complimentary products to sell throughout the year without having to do the work of creating the products and your customers will love you for it.

If you find 12 big players you can do mini product launches with each of them, one month at a time and always have something going on to grow your business. And when the customers finish one promotional cycle, you can now push them into other products and services that you receive an agreed upon commission on.

Here's a great example to help paint the picture in your mind. Let's say you find 6 great partners in your new product promotion network. On the first month everyone of the 6 sends traffic to your product in exchange for a commission on any sales. You make out like a bandit and so do your partners. They sent their customers to you because you are helping them solve a needed problem in the marketplace, like we discussed in the opening.

Then when month 2 rolls around everyone promotes the next guy. At the end of 6 months everyone had a turn, but you really won during all 6 months as you were selling your product to new customers that came to your store or website on the front end and collecting commission checks from your new network on the backend.

Using this strategy effectively is one of the most powerful networking tools you can put to use to grow your business and help people along the way. Your products and the products of your new product promotion network need to be A+ products that change lives and impact people.

When you do that, the world is yours.

ABOUT GREG

Greg Rollett, the ProductPro, works with authors, experts, entertainers, entrepreneurs and business owners all over the world to help them share their knowledge and change the lives and businesses of others. After creating a successful string of his own educational products, Greg began helping others in the production and marketing of their own products.

Previous clients include Coca-Cola, Miller Lite, Warner Bros and Cash Money Records as well as hundreds of entrepreneurs and small business owners. Greg's work has been featured on FOX News, ABC, the Daily Buzz and Greg has written for Mashable, the Huffington Post, AOL, AMEX's Open Forum and more.

Greg loves to challenge the current business environments that constrain people to working 12-hour days during the best portions of their lives. By teaching them to leverage technology and the power of information Greg loves helping others create freedom businesses that allow them to generate income, make the world a better place and live a radically ambitious lifestyle in the process.

A former touring musician, Greg is a highly sought after speaker having appeared on stages with former Florida Gov. Charlie Crist, best selling authors Chris Brogan and Nick Nanton as well as at events such as Affiliate Summit.

If you would like to learn more about Greg and how he can help your business, please contact him directly at greg@productprosystems.com or calling his office at 877.897.4611.

You can also download a free report on how to create your own educational products at www.productprosystems.com.